...COME IN, WHAT-EVER YOU ARE!!!

PUBLISHER'S DEDICATION

To The Mighty Ackermonster,
The Great FJA,
The star of 35 issues
(and still going strong)
of the magazine they said
couldn't be done.

He did it.

To Forry,
The Most Famous Monster
of them all,
This book is eternally Dedicated.

                                    J.W.

THEY SAID, IT COULDN'T BE DONE

THEY said you couldn't make a paperback book as great as *FAMOUS MONSTERS*.

THEY said it would only last one issue, the PTA (Peasants of Transylvania Association) would stop it.

THEY said, "How could you top it? Where would you get photos for the second book greater than the first?"

THEY said, "You can't do it! Impossible to come out with *SON OF FAMOUS MONSTERS!*"

THEY talk too much. THEM! What do they know about IT?

YOU — YOU are the ones we listen to, YOU thirsting thousands upon thousands who couldn't get enough Ghoul-Aid, Choke-late Sodas, Vanilla Milk-Shocks and Coca-Dracolas to soothe your parched throats till the glorious day (today) when you discover the *new FAMOUS MONSTERS STRIKE BACK!* on sale! Drink ye deep! Quench your thirst! Every page guaranteed to make your mouth water or your tongue replaced free of charge.

—Forrest J Ackerman
Editor,
Famous Monsters of Filmland Magazine

PAPERBACK LIBRARY EDITION

First Printing: June, 1965

Copyright © 1957, 1958, 1959, 1960, 1961, 1962, 1963, 1964, by Warren Publishing Company.

ALL RIGHTS RESERVED, including the right to reproduce this book or portions thereof.

This Paperback Library Edition was published by arrangement with Warren Publishing Company, Publishers of Famous Monsters of Filmland Magazine.

Paperback Library books are published by Paperback Library, Inc. Its trademark, consisting of the words "Paperback Library" and associated distinctive design, is registered in the United States Patent Office. Printed in the United States of America, Paperback Library, Inc., 260 Park Avenue South, New York, N.Y. 10010

JAMES WARREN
presents

FAMOUS

MONSTERS

OF FILMLAND

STRIKE BACK!

edited by

FORREST J ACKERMAN

THE
INCREDIBL

8

SHRINKER
OF MEN

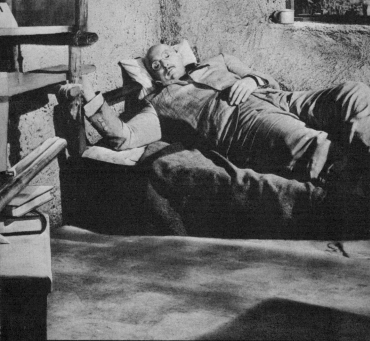

He took 5 normal people, this world's greatest authority on organic molecular structure, and turned them into a handful of shrunken heads—with shrunken bodies still attached and tiny hearts beating wildly in terror. To their doll-like eyes he was Gargantuan, until they blinded him in one eye and then he became—CYCLOPEAN!

The upper reaches of the Amazon, as every schoolboy from here to Pellucidar knows, is the domain of the Creature of the Black Lagoon. The lower reaches—ah, that's a different matter, and one we're about to explore via the great Paramount technicolor picture of 1940: DR. CYCLOPS.

On a forbidding knoll above the Karana River, at the headwaters of the mightly Amazon, is the mysterious experimental laboratory of Dr. Alexander Thorkel, rare civilized man in the Iquitos territory. The Peruvian natives thereabouts are suspicious and superstitious. The weird light and sounds that come from Thorkel's jungle retreat make the natives restless.

Thorkel gets guests

A scientific party arrives to be of assistance to the doctor (played by Albert Dekker with a Yul Brynner butch). They are:

Bill Stockton, mineralogist.

Dr. Rupert Bulfinch, biologist.

Mary Phillips, the biologist's assistant.

And Steve Baker, prospector looking for Inca gold who agrees to lead the other 3 to Thorkel.

man or devil?

And what of Thorkel himself—what impression did he make? Well, let us look at him thru the eyes of Charles Strong, who fictionized him in the book:

He might well have seemed to an ignorant native like someone akin to a demon. His burly body was completely encased from head to foot, when he worked (which was long, and late into the nite), in lead laboratory armor. When he looked out of his radioactive room while an experiment was in progress, his bare round face had an air of unreality about it. He looked (said the author) "like some great uncouth monster, whose eyes reflected the weird green light from the mica window."

little mistake, big trouble

The recently arrived foursome is only displaying normal scientific curiosity but Dr. Thorkel (who probably was a

Dr. Thorkel attempts to swat the miniature victims of his evil ray with the barrel of his gun.

little odd to begin with) seems to feel that they're poking their noses too much into his business. So he decides to shorten them. Not just their noses, but their whole bodies.

In short order, Bill, Mary, Dr. Bulfinch and Steve, plus Dr. Thorkel's man-of-all-work, Pedro, are hustled under the doc's shrinkoscope, and the next thing you know they're as small as 5 little all-day suckers!

In fact, they're so small that if they tried to lick a stamp, the stamp would probably lick them instead!

Mad doctor menaces miniature maiden in this moving scene.

technicians get in licks

Now comes the good part, the part that made the Special Effects wizards sweat. Most of you monster fans were around a couple of season ago when THE INCREDIBLE SHRINKING MAN was doing his stuff, and you remember how great that was. Or maybe you caught one of the telecasts of THE DEVIL DOLL, the A. Merritt chiller based on his book

Gotcha! One squeeze little man, and you'll feel like you were hit by the Atomic Palm!

Albert Dekker as Dr. Thorkel uses king-size monkey wrench on machine that makes men shrink.

"Burn Witch Burn!", in which the menace was on a miniature scale. Well, the illusion of littleness was very large in this flick, very large; like straight out of greatsville; like something described in Henry Hasse's "He Who Shrank" or Ray Cummings' "Girl in the Golden Atom" or Festus Pragnell's "Green Man of Kilsona" or Weaver Wright's "Micro-Man".

cat-astrophe

First off there's this cat, see, an evil feline named Satanas, that looks as large (and ferocious) as a sabre-tooth tiger to the little folk. It'd be no joke for any of them to meet up with this hungry tabby: one cat nip and they'd have had it! In one breath-taking sequence they cower in a cactus-forest as Satanas attacks them, their lives being saved when a dog about the size of a baby dinosaur scares the cat away.

14

Dr. Thorkel tries to persuade shrunken people to "Come up and see me sometime."

They're even menaced by a king-sized chicken that gives them a run for their money. Juvenile delinquent teenagers in later years did it with cars, but this sequence was probably the first film of *a chicken race*.

the greater alligator

But the worst is yet to come for the 5 man-nikins: they run into an alligator which, in their reduced circumstances, looks about as big as an atomic submarine!

Caught in the fury of a tropic thunderstorm, they are pelted by raindrops as big as bricks! As Henry Kuttner said at the time, "It was a rain of terror."

Every creeping, crawling, swimming, flying, *living* thing now is a potential source of danger to them, and even many inanimate objects can cause them fear.

job for jack giant-killer

What these wee ones really need is a friendly giant to sock the doc. They're pretty hampered with nothing much more to fight him with than a pin, a broken pair of scissors, and little things like that.

Once they *almost* get him with a shotgun, by pulling a string (big as a rope) attached to the trigger; but the moment, and the opportunity, pass.

Albert Dekker poses in his Sunday Asbestos suit while waiting for his guests to shrink.

"We hope to be as big as you are later, alligator!"

At last they get a desperate inspiration.

Dr. Thorkel is so dreadfully near-sighted that he once made a mistake and shaved the mirror instead of his face. For this reason he keeps a number of pairs of glasses handy around the lab. The midgets determine to hide all of them. They've just about got the job done when Thorkel wakes up. In an ensuing skirmish one lens gets smashed on his last pair.

Leaving him one-eyed.

17

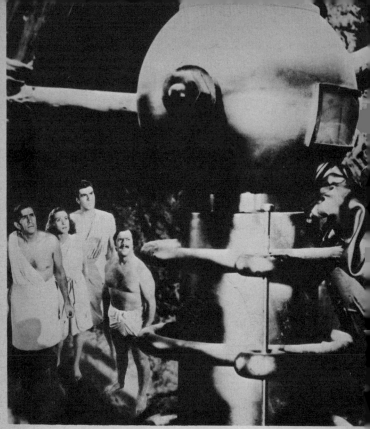

Four of the Pygmy people gaze in awe at the shrinking machine of Dr. Thorkel.

the mites and the mighty

Now it's war, war to the finish, between Cyclops and the teeny-agers.

Vision blurred, Thorkel goes berserk, shooting his gun, throwing furniture, turning the room topsy-turvy. In his near-blind rage he stumbles and falls into a well, but at the last moment clutches the rope on the windlass.

It is Steve Baker who risks his life to charge the Cyclops and make him fall to his death. The giant's day is done. Now he'll never create that army of little spies, subminiature saboteurs and "toy" soldiers that he had blueprinted in his brilliant but deranged brain. **END**

A final look at the face of the midget making fiend—Dr. Cyclops!

RETURN OF THE PHANTOM

by popular demand, many well-known monster and marvel movies have been remade. DONOVAN'S BRAIN, THE BAT, THE MYSTERIOUS ISLAND, DRACULA, FRANKENSTEIN, THE MUMMY, THE UNHOLY 3, to name a few. And so it was, in 1943, that THE PHANTOM OF THE OPERA was brought to life for the second time. Last issue you read in these pages how Lon Chaney played him—now turn back the clock 17 years to the time Claude Rains donned the Phantom Mask!

Claude Rains, as Erique Claudin, chokes Miles Mander in the 1943 movie version.

"The mad mob falls upon the madman and destroys him," we reported in FM #9 as we described the closing moments of the climax of the 1925 version: "Erik is no more. The Phantom has passed into legend."

Ah, but can you keep a good phantom down? Or a bad one?!

In the midst of World War II, the Phantom returned—a horror to take America's mind for a moment off horrors like Hitler and the Nazi Beasts.

return of the phantom

The remake of Gaston Leroux' PHANTOM OF THE OPERA was in Technicolor. It starred Claude Rains as the Phantom (known as Erique Claudin) and, it is interesting

It's no choke after the lady disfigures Erique with a pan of acid.

to note, featured one of the screen appearances of Fritz Leiber Sr, father of the Fritz Leiber Jr whose horror novel "Conjure Wife" was recently seen as a teleplay. Lon Chaney Sr, of course, starred in the original PHANTOM OF THE OPERA; and Lon Chaney Jr. starred in WITCH WOMAN, adapted from a novel by Fritz Leiber Jr. in a magazine called Unknown Worlds. Strange are the ways of Fate!

man into phantom

Erique Claudin was not born a monster, a cruel quirk of life turned him into one. For some years he was a respectable violinist in the orchestra of the Paris Opera, until his hands became crippled by arthritis and he could no longer perform. Though he had no job, he wanted to be able to pay for his

Claude Rains pulls his coat collar up around his throat and prepares for a long cold night of haunting in the catacombs.

Behind that mask is the face of a saint—a Saint Bernard! Doggone frightening, that's for sure.

daughter Christine to continue her voice-training exercises, and so he offered for sale his life's work, a piano concerto, to a publisher.

The unscrupulous publisher stole his score.

When Claudin learns of the theft, he is rightfully infuriated. Confronting the thief, he gets into a fight with him. Accidentally, the publisher is killed—and Claudin, disfigured for life when the publisher's secretary hurls acid in his face!

Mad with pain and seeking to escape the police, Claudin flees to the Paris Opera house and hides himself deep beneath the main floor in the maze of catacombs which honeycomb the dark acres of subterranean mystery.

Man no longer, pain and peril have turned him into a monster.

The acid has done more than eat away his face, it has corroded his brain. Erique Claudin is now mad. And the fires of his madness are fanned higher when he hears his stolen music being performed in the Opera!

Claudin sends a message to the manager of the Opera instructing him to replace his leading female singer with Christine. But the manager does not do as he says, and Claudin repeats with an enraged warning *demanding* that his daughter be given the principal singing role. When his warning is ignored, he makes good his threat.

The main chandelier, a heavy fixture of brittle glass hanging dangerously over the heads of the audience, sways as Claudin secretly manipulates it, and, suddenly, breaks loose from its fastening!

The great mass of glass plummets to the floor like an elevator with its cable cut!

Screams drown out the singers on the stage as innocent members of the audience are maimed and crushed in their seats, some turned in a terrifying instant to moaning bodies, others lifeless bloody corpses.

It is an awful thing the Phantom has done—and it is not the last.

the hands of erique

Like the Hands of Orlac, the hands of Erique now become killer's hands. For, when his further demands are flouted, he strangles first the chief female singer and then her maid! The musician's hands which once gently held a violin have become the violent instruments of murder.

His reason is now entirely gone. The Phantom kidnaps his own daughter. Christine is unaware that this horrible creature is her father for he hides his awful disfigurement behind a mask.

But in the picture's climax, Christine unmasks the scar-faced Claudin in a scene that brought screams as it did 18 years before. Although his make-up was nothing like Lon Chaney's, Claude Rains was a terrifying sight to behold, and not only did his daughter nearly faint, but all the faint-hearted people in the live theater audience!

end of the phantom?

In the nick of time, Christine's lover and a detective from the French Police track the Phantom to his lair and there poor demented Erique Claudin meets his end when a shot fired by the detective causes a cave-in of the age-weakened walls of the ancient catacombs . . .

His end?

Who can say for sure.

Lon Chaney and Claude Rains "died" in the role of the Phantom, but rumor hath it that the Phantom of the Opera, crushed to the earth, will rise again in 1961, courtesy of Hammer Productions of England. Who will he be—Christopher Lee? Anton Diffring? Lon Chaney Jr?

One thing's for certain: *FAMOUS MONSTERS'* faithful readers will be among the first human beings (?) in the world to get the facts!　　　　　　　　　　**END**

Claude Rains as The Phantom in "The Man Who Sawed Too Much."

Peter Lorre, the Warlock of Weirdom, (MAD LOVE) . . . 1935.

CALLING DR. CALIGARI

by Robert Bloch

Foreword: Exactly 10 years ago this summer the following cinemanalysis by Robert Bloch was published in a small subscription publication, FANTASTIC WORLDS, a literary quarterly of limited circulation devoted to the dissemination of fantasy articles & fiction. The editor, Sam Sackett, himself soon to become a selling science fiction author, said in introducing the article: "Anyone who has ever read any science fiction or fantasy is familiar with the name of Robert Bloch, whose protean productivity, beginning at the age of 17, is astounding. The high level of his writing can best be seen by dipping into his collection of short stories, 'The Opener of the Way'. In this article he shows himself a wide scholar and discriminating critic of cinematic horror."

The CABINET OF DR. CALIGARI (1919).

29

the greeks had a weird for it

According to ancient Greek legend, when Pandora opened the box, a lot of troubles were loosed on the world.

According to modern fact, when fat pudgy old Doc Caligari opened up his cabinet he loosed somnambulist Cesare and—with him—an unending wave of so-called "horror movies."

So-called.

That's where the troubles begin—troubles that made Pandora's brood look pretty sickly in comparison.

Ever since THE CABINET OF DR. CALIGARI was released, the movie-makers have devoted themselves to the fairly frequent fabrication of fantasy. Said fantasy has ranged from the cartoon ghoulishness of Mr. Disney to the pseudorealism of the Swiss THE ETERNAL MASK.

And, as is the case in literature, each effort is hailed by some, denounced by others. Everybody, it seems, reacts differently to cinematic shockers. Everybody has his own opinions. This, of course, is what makes horse-racing. But does it make "horror movies"?

My contention, synthesized in scholarly summation, is— *uh-uh*. It doesn't. It makes everything else but.

insipid sequels

It makes KING KONG and then SON OF KONG burlesquing its predecessor. It concocts FRANKENSTEIN and then adds Abbott & Costello. It gives us 3 successive DRACULAS—Lugosi, Junior Chaney & Carradine; then throws in a daughter for good measure. It knocks out a HOUSE OF HORRORS with Louise Fazenda & Chester Conklin, just for laffs, and fails to provide said silent epic with any humor. It goes to great lengths to do & re-do DR. JEKYLL & MR. HYDE and concentrate on a non-existent series of love affairs which a poor hack like Stevenson didn't have the sense to write into his story.

upchuck, son of chuck

So the producers & power-that-be prefer to operate that way. So it's their business. So let them. But meanwhile, they accompany these gyrations with a steady barrage of attendant adjectives. *"Chilling, Thrilling, Horrible, Not for Weak Hearts, You'll Gasp, You'll Scream, You'll Throw Up—"*

That last is granted.

But the rest is obfuscation. If the movie-makers think

they are turning out "horror movies" they are mistaken. If the movie-goers think they are attending "horror movies" they are mistaken. So much nonsense has poured out of Caligari's cabinet in the last 30-odd years that it's difficult

DEAD OF NIGHT—1946—qualifies as Bloch's " almost perfect" horror film.

for either movie-maker or movie-goer to remember just what it is they're talking about.

The purely arbitrary conventions & stylizations surrounding the production of fantasy have made it difficult to criticize the cinema unless an attempt is made to define basic terms.

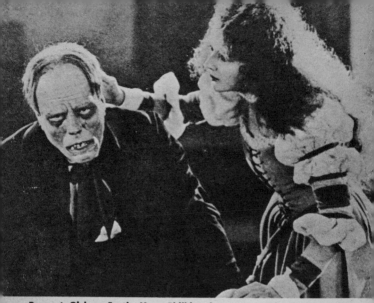

Bravest Girl on Earth, Mary Philbin, shows compassion for Erik, the Most Horrifying Man on Earth in THE PHANTOM OF THE OPERA.

the sixty-fear holler question

So—what's a "horror movie"?

A horror movie is (a) a film (b) whose content horrifies. Simple? Obvious? Yes. But remember, we're operating in a strange frame of reference. We're dealing with movie-makers who are more interested in the icing of adjectives than they are in the actual contents of the cake. As long as they shout "Devil's Food!" loud enough they think the public will swallow it.

And most of the movie-going public, having never tasted actual horror fare, do just that. To many, the clutching hand & the body falling out of the closet, the shadow on the wall & the guy in the moth-eaten ape costume, constitute the epitome of terror-in-celluloid. They accept the convention of "comic relief" and know by heart every cliche.

the shape of things:

Which leaves the true *aficionados* only a few crumbs. Because, as I stated previously, in my opinion there are no true "horror movies"— motion pictures designed purely & simply to scare the devil out of you.

The climax of the classic FRANKENSTEIN. Karloff watches anxiously as villagers prepare to set fire to the mill in which he has taken refuge.

33

There are, instead, "trick" movies & "science fiction" movies & "mystery thrillers" & "comedy mysteries" & standard items featuring "Karloff the Fiend" (in which Karloff invariably portrays the role of a kindly white-haired old scientist with a beautiful daughter, his "fiendishness" being limited to a misguided attempt to conduct an advanced "scientific experiment").

sweeping statement

Alright, then, let's sweep up the crumbs & see what we can find there.

Here, from the breadbox of memory, are a few crumby moments of "pure horror" I've found in films.

1. The sequence in Val Lewton's THE CAT PEOPLE where the train suddenly rushes over the trestle . . . followed, a few moments later, by the trickle of blood under a doorway.

2. Peter Lorre coming up the stairs with the fake steel neck, in his first American movie, MAD LOVE.

3. Lorre again, in the little-known RKO effort THE STRANGER ON THE THIRD FLOOR—specifically, in the dream sequence.

4. Conrad Veidt's somnambulistic sortie in the aforementioned CABINET OF DR. CALIGARI.

5. Veidt, again, in Paul Leni's production of WAX-WORKS.

6. The single shot in KING KONG where the giant ape's head peers thru the windows of the wrecked el train, his eyeballs rolling hideously.

7. Lon Chaney at the organ in THE PHANTOM OF THE OPERA.

8. The scene where the armless, legless monstrosity crawls thru the mud, knife in teeth, in Tod Browning's FREAKS.

9. Lionel Atwill's scene in THE MYSTERY OF THE WAX MUSEUM where the waxen mask is ripped away from his burned face.

10. Basil Rathbone's brief sequence at the piano in an otherwise hopeless Paramount turkey, titled (and this will give you some idea of the whole) THE MAD DOCTOR.

11. The last sequence in the British DEAD OF NIGHT where the entire film dissolves into a kaleidoscopic montage of imagery. (By the way, DEAD OF NIGHT comes closer to being a true "horror film" than almost any other nominee, in my opinion.)

34

PETER LORRE

JOHN McGUIRE

Lorre's dream sequence in this one gave Bloch daymares.

12. The ghost-voice echoing thru the house in THE UNINVITED.

13. One solitary shot in the original DRACULA: Bela Lugosi descends the cobwebbed stairs of the castle & approaches the commercial traveler.

14. The "shock" moment of GREAT EXPECTATIONS when Finlay Currie as the convict rises up out of nowhere to confront the boy in the graveyard.

15. The sequences involving the dead Edith Evans in the British production of THE QUEEN OF SPADES.

These are the moments I remember—the ones that yanked me out of my seat. All too often the films as a whole merely yanked me out of the theater.

But one man's meat is another man's poison. So if you don't agree with my findings—tell me, what *did* poison you? **END**

FOR IT

AGAIN DR. ACULA descends into the depths to dig up sequestered fotos. "If they're not what YOU requested," he states, "it's all my vault for not wearing my moon glasses." Make your wants known to DR. AX at 1426 E. Washington Lane, Philadelphia 38, Pa.

A rare action scene of the attack of the Animal Men in George Pal's ATLANTIS, for TAD JOHNSTONE, BRYCE PELZ & ROGER HAMM.

The man covered with the Mystery Substance for ENEMY FROM SPACE (Quatermass II) for CURTIS MASEMORE of Denison, Texas, and MICHAEL MORRISON of San Antonio, Tex.

For DON BENNETT, JON BERRY, OLLIE PARKER and other CHRIS LEE fans, this foto from THE MUMMY (1959).

For BEN SLATER, LEN CHAPMAN & TOD CARNELL the star with the scar-face from CIRCUS OF HORRORS: ANTON DIFFRING.

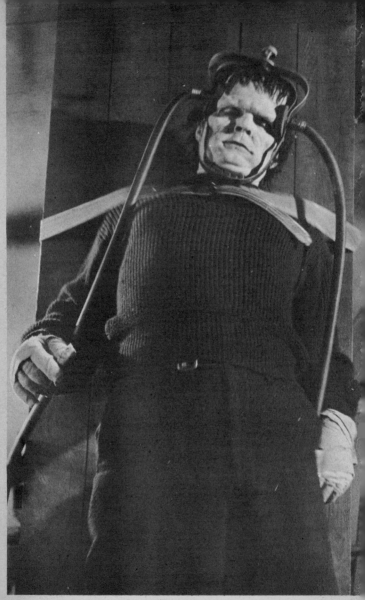

An extremely rare photo of a Frankenstein Monster most people have never seen—DON MEGOWAN as The Monster in the Hammer Films TV series TALES OF FRANKENSTEIN for TOMMY MORAN and MICHAEL BANKS.

Another great role played by **CHRISTOPHER LEE:** the Vampiric Count in **HORROR OF DRACULA,** requested by **MARY CAHILL, CHICK BARR, CLAIR HELDING, ALLIS VILLETTE & BELLE CRIDLAND.**

Ricky McCammon of Birmingham, Alabama wanted us to compare the scenes showing Quasimodo on the whipping post—from THE HUNCHBACK OF NOTRE DAME—in each of the three movies that were made from this great classic. Above, the most recent, with Anthony Quinn as The Hunchback. Opposite page (top): the immortal Lon Chaney in the original 1923 version. Bottom: James Cagney recreates the life of Lon in MAN OF 1,000 FACES.

43

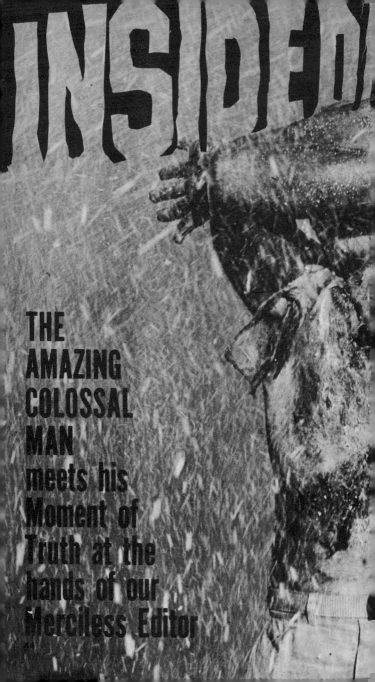

INSIDE

THE
AMAZING
COLOSSAL
MAN
meets his
Moment of
Truth at the
hands of our
Merciless Editor

RKESTACULA

Who wins in THE COLOSSAL BEAST? Producer or public? Decide for yourself!

45

He's bombed . . . he's burned . . . he's about to become COLOSSAL!

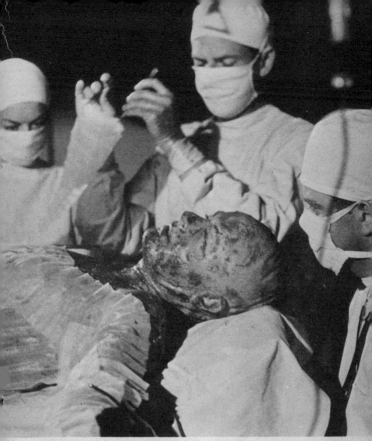

His life at stake on the operating table.

big hand for colossal man

I think you will enjoy this picture. I did. I saw the preview of it together with Edmond Hamilton, whose "Pigmy Island" I sold for filming to Sol (Tarzan) Lesser. "Pigmy Island" had something in common with DR. CYCLOPS and was described as "a powerful, vivid, super-science tale of tiny men and giant rats and snakes" when it was first published in *WEIRD TALES* magazine.

Hamilton liked THE AMAZING COLOSSAL MAN better than THE INCREDIBLE SHRINKING MAN. Altho I preferred Richard Matheson's screenplay to the scenario created by Bert Gordon & Mark Hanna, considering COLOSSAL MAN cost but a fraction of SHRINKING MAN it certainly was worth complimenting.

giant's acting packs punch

Much of the picture's power is derived from the performance of Glen Langan as the Giant. He does an excellent job. Langan plays Col. Glen Manning, victim of a freak accident during the detonation of the first plutonium bomb. In a heroic effort to save another man's life, it at first appears that Col. Manning has lost his own when the blast sears every inch of skin from his body. The scene where he is charred before the camera's eye by the atomic radiation is a hair raiser and is effectually reprised twice during the unfoldment of the film.

Burned bald from head to toe, dehydrated and at death's door, Manning is given no chance to survive the night. But the next morning his skin has miraculously grown back and his metabolism is nearly normal! Instead of a scarred corpse he appears to be a convalescent on the way to complete recovery! The baffled doctors can only conclude that plutonium rays must have some marvelous powers to effect recuperation.

The trouble sets in, of course, when Manning not only recuperates but *starts to grow*. At the rate of 8 to 10′ a day. Dr. Listrom explains the phenomenon to Manning's fiancee, Carol: 'As you probably already know, the body is like a factory. Continually producing new cells to replace the older cells, damaged cells, or destroyed cells. This happens in all the different parts of the body. Bone cells grow new bone cells, skin cells grow new skin cells and so on—" Co-doctor Coulter continues with the explanation: "It is this delicately balanced process of new cells replacing dying cells that is causing the growth problem. The process is out of balance. For some unknown reason, new cells are growing at an accelerated or speeded-up rate—" and right here I want to stop the dialog to direct your attention to something I consider significant. Note that usage, "accelerated or speeded-up"; the basic English form describing the more "difficult" word in case there's anyone in the audience who doesn't understand it. I noticed this happening so many times in the picture that it formed a pattern. "A stimulus," someone would say, adding "or force" in case a simpler word was required to communicate to a watcher of the film what a stimulus was.

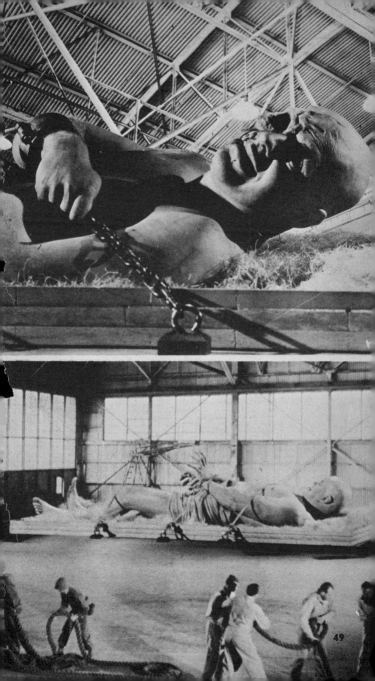

how to kill a giant

Now of course at this point one good modern Technical Adviser could have stepped in and, if listened to, stopped the giant dead in his tracks. He would say. "They could get away with more when Wells wrote 'Food of the Gods' or 'The Nth Man' first appeared (1928)," and then go to destroy the possibility of an artificial giant altogether by pointing out that, like a dinosaur, he'd have to spend practically all his time eating, that his bones couldn't support his weight, etc.

Spoilsport!

The impossible AMAZING COLOSSAL MAN is about 80′ tall before he's thru and has taken giant steps thru downtown Las Vegas, doing more damage than the one-armed bandits.

The AMAZING COLOSSAL MAN meets his (apparent)

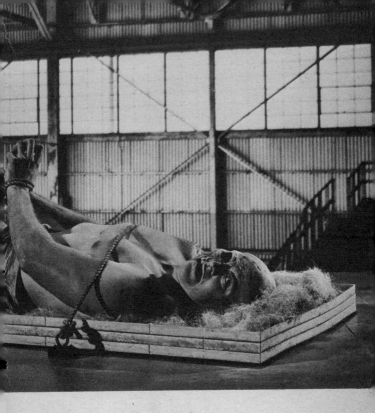

doom at Boulder Dam but the clink of coins at a healthy box-office can often work wonders in reviving the deadest of monsters so let's put it this way: I wouldn't be amazed to learn of a sequel.

I was right!

Run for the hills, folks, THE COLOSSAL BEAST is coming!

The Beast is the sequel to THE AMAZING COLOSSAL MAN. While shooting, it was first known as *The Return of the Colossal Man* and, later, *The Revenge of the Colossal Man*.

I got the story of the sequel from Bert Gordon, who wrote & produced it, on the set of the picture while the final scenes were being shot. The Colossal Man was going thru

his King-like performance of swatting at a gnat-like model plane. His make-up was reminiscent of the giant in one of Gordon's previous pictures, CYCLOPS.

WAR OF THE COLOSSAL BEAST opens with a brief, breathless sequence before the title & credits come on the screen, of a terrified Mexican boy racing a truck away from some unseen thing that is pursuing him. The thing is unseen but—not unheard: a great drumbeat of footsteps penetrates the roar of the engine and the screech of the tires. When the car goes out of control the boy runs for his life down an empty stream bed till he stumbles & falls and a black shadow envelopes him as the title appears.

Picture proper opens with an American named Swanson reporting the theft of his truck to the police sergeant in a little Mexican village. The boy who "stole" the truck is soon located across the street in a doctor's office—in a state of shock. He is no more help than was the little girl in THEM! who had seen the gi-ants.

The car owner, accompanied by the policeman, goes to the spot where the boy was found. But his car is not around. The policeman observes that "It looks like the car went

straight up in the air, senor!" At which Swanson snorts, "It was equipped with heater and radio but it didn't have wings." And later that day, in the news, a telecaster reporting the incident of the truck that "flew away" jokes: "Well, the birds grow pretty big in Mexico.

impossible theory

Joyce Manning, sister of the Colossal Man, tho she believes him dead has a hunch about the mysterious happening in Mexico and gets hold of Swanson. In her apartment in Beverly Hills, California, she introduces Swanson to Col. Baird. The possibility that her brother is still alive is brought up by Joyce but the brass considers it utterly impossible: "Believe me—and all the medical authorities agree—no man, even if he was 60' tall, could take those two bazooka charges and fall over Boulder dam and live. The drop alone —over 700'—would kill him."

Disappointed but undaunted, Joyce goes to Mexico to see the boy. She sits by Miguel's side during the nite. He murmurs: "HOMBRON!" What does it mean? "It is hard to say," the doctor says; "a great big fellow, like an ogre in a story. A monster, a giant man..."

fantastic reality

Before long it is established that the Colossal Manning is alive and a plan to drug him with chloral hydrate impregnated bread is effected. Captured, and in a comatose state, he is transported across the border back to the States, where his fate is the same from here to finis as the brontosaurus of THE LOST WORLD, old Kong himself, the Venusia ymir that THE TWENTY MILLION MILES TO EARTH, and all other unfortunate beasts that grow too big for their bridges: he's destroyed till nextime. Altho this time it looks like he's really cooked (and in color, for the final few seconds), as the script reads: *The Colossal Man puts out a hand towards the power lines, then lunges at them suddenly. The current flows thru his body, visibly, turning his flesh the color of molten steel. For a long beat, he hangs there in the air, burning, turning white, glowing. His flesh & muscle burn away and he is an incandescent skeleton in the night. Then even his bones are calcified to ash, and as they drop in powder to a glowing heap on the ground, we superimpose on the quiet night sky*:

THE END.

Of the *ash*tounding Colossal Man.

Farewell, Cruel World!

the clown at midnite

#4 in Our Series on Imaginative Movies

HORROR IS MY BUSINESS.

The insurance agent peddles protection & security—I sell terror & dread. The doctor guards your heart; I devote my professional skill to inducing failure in same. Some people live by their wits; I live by scaring you out of yours.

For the past 27 years I've been a professional writer of *horror fiction for magazines, books, radio and TV shows. And when I'm not creating nightmares of my own, I spend my spare time investigating the nightmares of other people—namely the so-called "horror" movies· being foisted off on the public via TV and theater screens. —*

ROBERT BLOCH.

It used to be, back in the bad old depression days when apples were sold on street corners and cars had rumble seats, that the horror film was practically an art-form as well as being almost as hot at the box-office as Bank Night. The

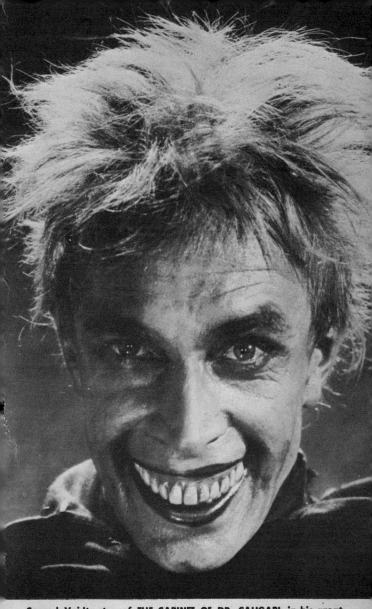

Conrad Veidt, star of THE CABINET OF DR. CALIGARI, in his great role (1928) as THE MAN WHO LAUGHS, from the novel by Victor Hugo.

Count Dracula is lured by the sight of his favorite drink (blood) pouring from a cut on the hand of Dwight Frye.

terror tale was filmed with more Tender Loving Care than Pres. Johnson gets at Walter Reed Hospital, and imaginative producers never forgot for a moment that the viewer had an imagination of his own.

Unfortunately, for better or for worse, the folklore of the land is changing. Just as Halloween, with its ghosts & goblins, has been transformed into a sub-teen Thanks-giving with Tricks-or-Treats replacing the turkey, so has the horror movie suffered a sea-change into something strictly for laffs, with genuine grue & imagination being replaced by a vat of ketchup and a false face that wouldn't frighten a timid two-year-old.

The shudder salesmen have sold out and the average horror flick nowadays evokes more gaiety than goose-pimples.

But it boots no good to shed melancholy tears over the fright films of our youth that populated our dark and lonely bedrooms with images of Frankenstein's Monster and the Mummy gibbering just beyond the counterpane. It's more instructive, perhaps, to look into the reason why the morbid has been changed into the unintentionally mirthful.

Much as we dislike to consider it, one answer keeps cropping up: Hollywood no longer knows what horror is.

what's more horrifying

We could get philosophical at this point and wonder if it's really that simple or if it's just that people can't be horrified anymore. A casual glance at any paper will prove that the monsters currently roaming a city's streets after dark are far

Lon Chaney Jr. snarls once more as Larry (The Wolfman) Talbot in this scene from HOUSE OF FRANKENSTEIN.

This is one of thousands of sketches made before the actual shooting of the saga of the fifty story simian—KING KONG.

more horrible, in one sense, than anything Hollywood has yet dreamed up. And it was not too long ago that human beings were eliminated by the carload lots in the gas chambers of Belsen & Dachau—certainly the pinnacle of horror as far as human history goes. In addition, everybody reading this is probably painfully aware (tho none of us like to think about it) that all somebody has to do is push the wrong button and half of humanity will go up in smoke & radioactive ashes.

But all of this—while certainly horrible to contemplate—is not true *horror* as such. Horror is something peculiar to the individual.

horror is—

—a small child's (and quite frequently an adult's!) fear of the dark ... and most particularly the phantoms of the

Menacing Fredric March (as Mr. Hyde) is about to attack Rose Hobart in this scene from the 1932 version of DR. JEKYLL AND MR. HYDE.

imagination that populate the dark.

   —the fear of a human being who doesn't act, think or a look like a human being.

   —the fear of deformity

   —insanity

   —and even (far more pathetically) the fear of a cerebral palsy victim. (There, but for the grace of God . . .)

It's the fear of spiders & snakes and the pale horrors you find under rocks in the woods.

The fear of the Unknown

. . . the unexpected

. . . the not-quite-seen.

the height of horror

When *I* was an 8-year-old I saw Lon Chaney in THE PHANTOM OF THE OPERA—and gazed upon the face of naked fear. A couple of years ago I attended a revival of the same film. And despite the flickering flaws of this dated melodrama, the scene where Chaney is unmasked exerted the same monstrous magic upon a modern audience.

Since the 1925 version of THE PHANTOM, Hollywood has arrayed itself in noseputty & fright-wig hundreds of times. And yet only a score of genuinely shivery efforts have actually emerged from the studios (and practically none since World War II.)

During the '30s the movie moguls outdid themselves and gave us DRACULA, a FRANKENSTEIN, a MUMMY and a WOLF MAN, and even a few fairly respectable sequels. And then some pillow-head decided that since is was such a thin line between horror & hilarity, why not erase the line altogether? The integrity of the horror film was quickly corrupted and the honest seeker after shudders was lured into a back alley inhabited by Abbott & Costello and the Bowery Boys. Just about the time Frankenstein was due to meet Pa & Ma Kettle, some giddy genius discovered liquid latex and the "monster film" was born. (Frankenstein's Monster, we'll admit, may have been the first of these but the horror depended on far more than just a fright face with high forehead, dank hair, scars, and two collar studs projecting from the neck).

the bad bugs from empty space

Things began emerging from Outer Space—or the equally empty regions between a producer's ears. The screens of the nation were invaded by a horde of Giant Cockroaches &

Lon Chaney as Quasimodo the demented and malformed bellringer of the 1923 classic, HUNCHBACK OF NOTRE DAME.

Henry Hull as the original hairy horror—THE WEREWOLF OF LONDON.

The standard and the censored version of FRANKENSTEIN. The rare scene below shows the Monster throwing the little girl in the water in the mistaken notion that she, like the daisies, will float.

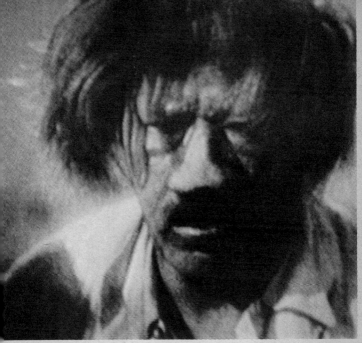

One of the "manimals" created on THE ISLAND OF LOST SOULS by Dr. Moreau in the Paramount production of 1932 from the story by HGWells, script by Philip Wylie.

Giant Bedbugs (all of which warmed the hearts of the pest-exterminators at the same time they cooled the ardor of the true horror fan.)

That these not-so-Grand Guignol efforts make money is undeniable. Vast audiences still watch the tired old travesties on television and turn out for each new double feature. But if producers believe these films show a profit because this is what the public really wants, let's face it—audiences lap up their pictures only because nothing better is available.

meaning of fear forgotten

While today's films prove that Hollywood has progressed in the use of camera tricks, animation, miniature photography and make-up, they also prove a total ignorance of what inspires the release of fear. One of the best examples is a produced-in-Japan flick (an American outfit later picked it up and dubbed in some English dialog and narrator in the person of Raymond Burr, currently popular as TV's Perry Mason) called GODZILLA. The *piece de resistance* of the film is a 10-story monster that cheerfully tears apart the city of Tokyo, evoking all kinds of admiration for the experts who built the miniature sets but no true feeling of horror on the part of the audience. (As von Clausewitz is reputed to have said, "One death is a tragedy, a million are statistics."

On the other hand, an excellent example of true horror in a film is the sight of one dwarfed, armless and legless torso crawling thru the mud in an old movie called FREAKS. This scene was enough to raise the hackles of the most sophisticated audience.

"Power to rule . . . to make the World grovel at my feet!"—Claude Rains as THE INVISIBLE MAN.

Paul Wagner as the living statue of clay known as THE GOLEM (1920).

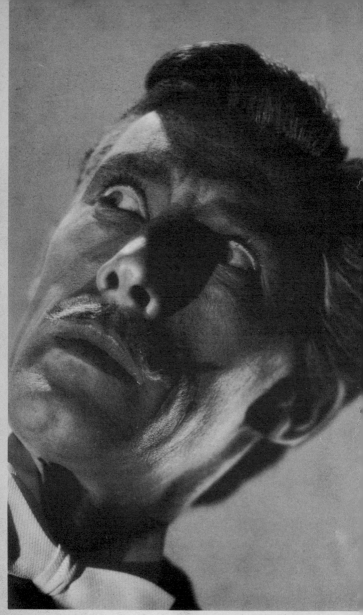

A formal portrait of John Carradine as the immortal Vampire—Count Dracula.

The Battle of the Titans—Kong prepares to challenge the mighty Tyranosaurus Rex for supremacy of Skull Island.

Of course, film producers are not-entirely to blame—they have been influenced by the censors who have curiously limited the size of the canvas upon which the horror film producers can paint. The censor who were not happy with the "morbidity" of FREAKS were singularly undisturbed when walls of fire toppled upon helpless thousands in WAR OF THE WORLDS. One lone ripper-murderer tempts the censorial blue-pencil far more than a BEAST FROM 20,000 FATHOMS whose poisonous presence perils an entire city. A BEAST is entirely moral in his relationships with women and is content to merely trample them to death.

the horrors of censorship

Let's look at a few of the better examples of horror films and see what the censors have done—or undone.

After 30 years of repetition & burlesque, it is hardly probable that an audience can view the original FRANKENSTEIN and recapture its initial impact. It's even less likely if they catch bits and pieces of it sandwiched in between drandruff & deodorant commercials on a 21″ tube.

But in its day FRANKENSTEIN qualified as a true tale of terror. Its theme, "The Monster is loose!", is still the basis of most so-called "science fiction" movies today. The first few scenes of the shambling monstrosity walking backwards or stumbling around the castle convey a genuine sense of the unearthly.

There are, or were originally, *two* versions of FRANK-

Scientist Rotwang and his creation, the robotrix, in a scene from the immortal classic METROPOLIS.

ENSTEIN. In the one generally shown and currently revived on TV, the Monster befriends a little girl on a river bank and watches her toss flowers into the water, petal by petal. There is an abrupt cutaway from the scene and when next we see the girl she is dead, being carried into town by her stunned father.

Glen Strange as Frankenstein's Monster appears almost as frightening in HOUSE OF FRANKENSTEIN as did Boris Karloff in the original
version of Mary Wollstonecraft Shelley's classic tale of terror.

"When I saw Lon Chaney as THE PHANTOM OF THE OPERA, I gazed upon the face of naked fear."—Robert Bloch

the unseen frankenstein

In the banned version, the flower-tossing episode is continued and the Monster, not out of cruelty but merely thru confusion, picks up the child and tosses her into the water. He is too ignorant to understand; if the pretty petals looked even prettier when they floated, why not a pretty girl?

The censors thought otherwise, apparently. They would rather cut the scene and leave the far more ghastly inference. The true horror is thus discarded in favor of a sordid situation immediately identifiable by the newspaper-reading public.

they done our kong wrong...

In KING KONG, another genuine all-out horror fantasy, there is a scene where the giant ape, loose in New York, holds the squirming body of a man between his huge teeth. The censors left this alone but they removed a scene where the same ape picks away at the heroine's garments out of mere curiosity.

Karloff the King in the role that won him immortality—the Frankenstein Monster.

They also eliminated the scene where Kong, searching for the heroine, plucks a girl from her hotel room and then, realizing he has made a mistake, drops her to the street below. Gruesome? Yes, but it *is*, after all, a horror movie. (In this case, of course, the horror lies in the utter casualness with which Kong drops her). And I can't quite comprehend why a censor would scissor this out and retain the graphic closeup of a man screaming between the clenched teeth of a 60′ gorilla.

The same film contained a sequence where members of the exploring party are eaten by a sea-monster and dashed to death in a chasm. The chasm scene conclusion, where some of them are devoured by giant spiders, was excised. (It would seem that the capricious censors are also dieticians; seamonsters can eat men but spiders cannot).

COMING UP SOON —wherein you will read what Mr. Bloch has to say about Boris Karloff & Lon Chaney Jr., Bela Lugosi & Peter Lorre, DR. JEKYLL & MR. HYDE, THE CAT PEOPLE, DEAD OF NIGHT, DIABOLIQUE, THE THING, THE UNINVITED and the weird episode in THREE CASES OF MURDER. **END**

WAY OUT

HUNG
BACK

Quasimodo writhes again!
A Special Feature—by the
Make-up Artist himself— Dick Smith

DICK SMITH (Left) applying his masterpiece of TV make-up for THE FALSE FACE.

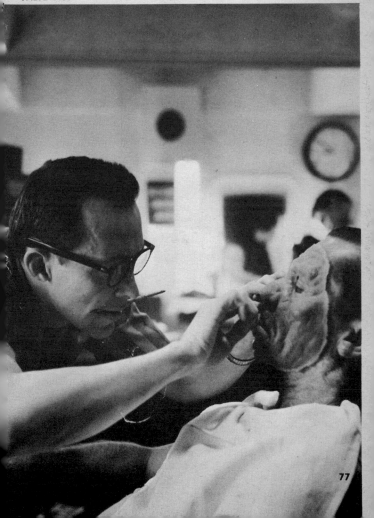

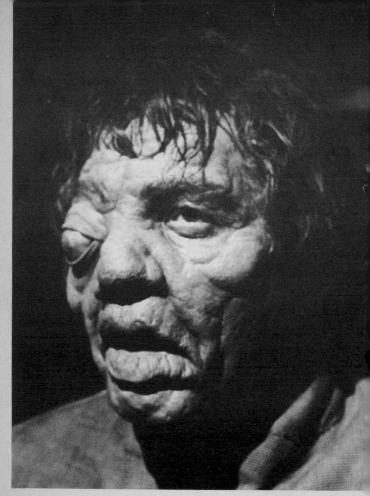

DEAD EYE DICK. This version of Smith's make-up was considered too gruesome eye-wise.

WAY OUT went out of its way to be gruesomely realistic when Roald Dahl presented the *Face in the Mirror* episode of his weekly terrorvision program. In it an actor, recreating on the legitimate stage the role of the Hunchback of Notre Dame, copied the hideous features of an unfortunate derelict ... then found he couldn't rub the face of horror off!

Two weeks before the show was taped, I was given a copy of the script to read. After finishing it I prepared some

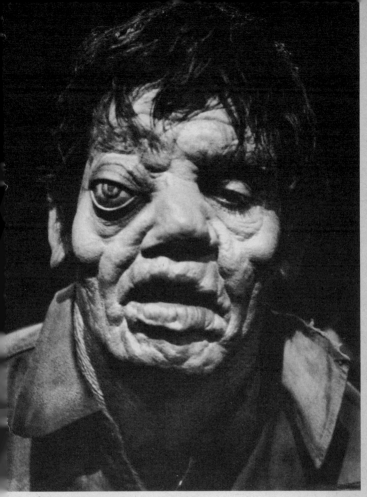

MARTIN "BUM" BROOKS in the "less gruesome" version of the mask that was used on WAY OUT.

rough sketches of what I felt the fatal face should look like: fairly grotesque but eyes nearly normal. However, after viewing my drawings the producer didn't think the face was "way out" enough. My next stop was a large personal library.

I studied a number of volumes in the extensive collection of medical text books belonging to a friend of mine—works dealing with tumors, facial diseases, plastic surgery, etc., with

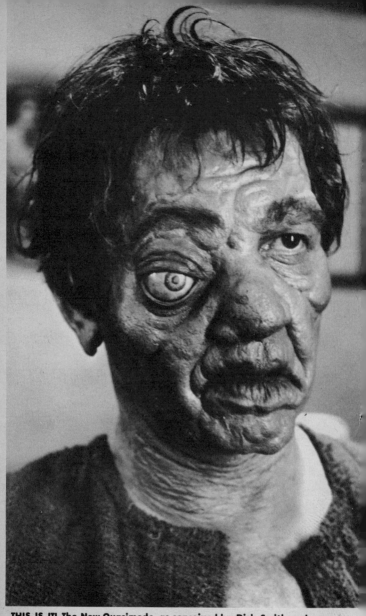

THIS IS IT! The New Quasimodo, as conceived by Dick Smith and seen on Roald Dahl's show.

accompanying photographs—and came away convinced that no make-up artist can improve on the horrors of nature. Nevertheless, I tried. I designed a leprosy-like face, puffy of cheek & jowl, with thickened lips. To this attractive beginning I added a weird scar and a bulging eye, and—*voila!*—after only about 120 hours of construction I completed the mask.

First I made a life mask of Alfred Ryder, who played the part of the actor who played the hunchback. That took

ROUGH SKETCH COMES FIRST

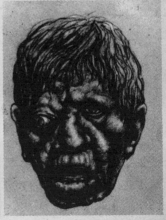

THE UNHOLY 3—Smith's original sketches for fearsome face of the 'Way Out Hunchback.

ALFRED RYDER AS "The Actor", man who copied another man's face to perfection plus!

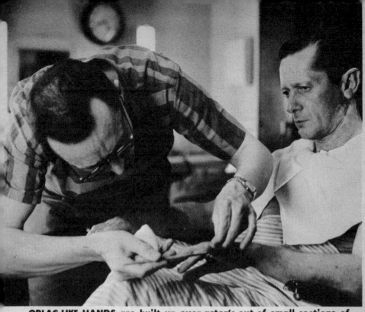

ORLAC-LIKE HANDS are built up over actor's out of small sections of "living" latex.

COTTON THE ACT! Dick Smith glues thin layer of cotton to throat of uncomfortable actor.

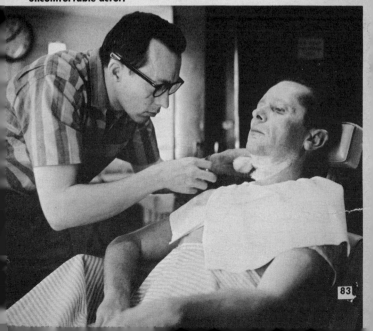

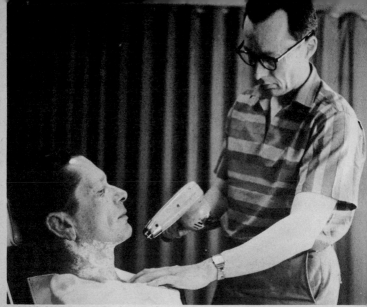

DICK SMITH APPLIES layer of special glue in order to make horror mask stick.

WITH SHAGGY WIG added, made-up man is about ready to take a look at himself.

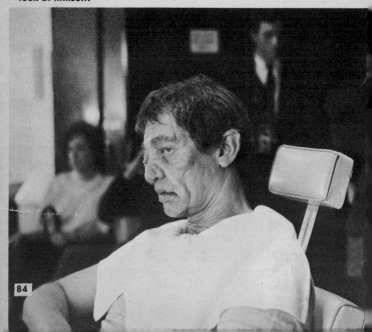

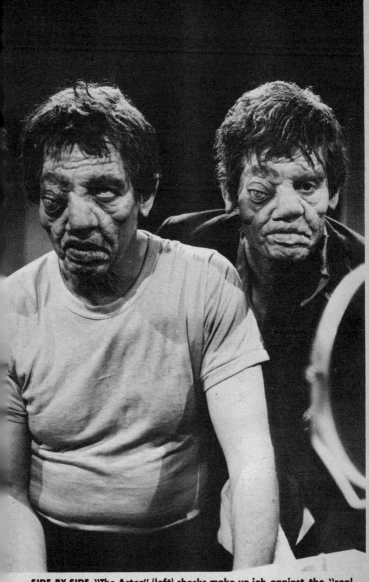

SIDE BY SIDE. "The Actor" (left) checks make-up job against the "real thing" (right).

nearly a week, then the eye had to be modified as the producer felt it "a bit too much" for TV. I then designed the *same* mask for the "bum." In other words, we had 2 plaster faces which looked just like each actor's natural face, and on top of them the distorted mask was fashioned of modeling clay: new eyes, nose, cheeks, mouth, etc. The second "skin" had to be kept as thin as possible to allow the actors facial mobility.

From the second clay model, a plaster mold was made. When removed from the life mask and model, the clay was all carefully cleaned away, then foam latex churned up in something like an eggbeater and heated. The resultant goo was poured into the "negative" half of the mold. Then the life mask, which had been made to fit into the mold, was pushed back into it. The 2 pieces were united, foam latex inside, and as soon as the latex jelled it was put into an oven and—baked!

don't half-bake

(A word of caution to do-it-yourself mask-makers: an underdone mask can be as disastrous as the Bride of Frankenstein's first custard pie, so if you're baking your own be sure to "cure" the latex for 3 hours. After the heat treatment, remove from the mold and trim surplus edges.)

Due to lack of time on the 'WAY OUT play, I had to fashion the hideous eye out of *dental* supplies rather than have a proper glass one prepared. In the show, when the actor was supposed to remove the make-up (which, as explained, was really a mask), he accidentally hit the artificial eye with a modeling stick and it popped right out! But it happened so quickly that no one—not even the technicians in the control room—noticed. The producer decided 99 out of 100 viewers wouldn't catch this accident so the mishap was telecast as taped.

a gimmick a day ain't hay

In one important sequence the actor took out a jar of cold cream, applied putty to his nose, added eyes, and so forth— and this had to be done without stopping the cameras. On the telescreen it took 90 seconds. His secret: a gimmick with the clay. First, 10 seconds of someone's hand (that was supposed to be his) was on the screen, then the actor would be seen via another camera, putting the putty on his

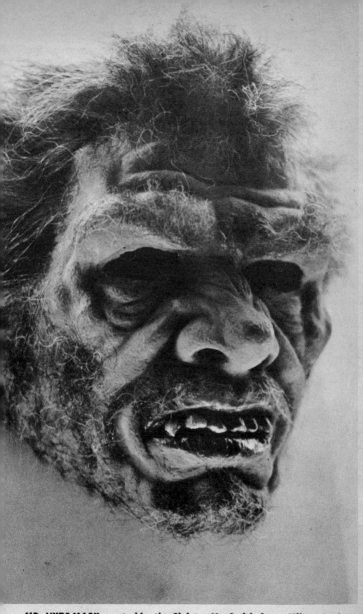

MR. HYDE MASK created by the Sinister Mr. Smith for a Milton Berle tele-ghast.

THE DEVIL'S GRANDMA! Another Satanic Make-up created by Devilish Dick, who'll be back in our pages soon with another revealing feature on "The Art of Making Fiends and Influencing People"!

nose. Back to the first camera for the hands picking up some tool or anything to take up 20 seconds while the actor would hastily drop the piece of putty and grab a previously prepared section of the mask that covered nose & lips. This portion of make-up, already wet with glue, would readily stick to his face mask. Ryder would put it over his nose & mouth, then pick up a modeling stick and pretend to be finishing the edges. The TV eye would record this action; then a cutback to the first camera and the bit of business with the hands: maybe the fingers would be carving an eyeball this time. While camera No. 2 was busy with the hands, the actor would grab another section of the mask—and so on until the completed mask was on his face.

make-up take-off

After he had supposedly worn his Hunchback make-up on stage, the actor (in the story) returned to his dressing-room to remove the monster face—only to discover to his horror that he couldn't! Not even the surface make-up came off this time. The problem was to have the actor wrestle with the mask, trying to remove his face, but not have any of the make-up come loose as that would disastrously spoil the illusion, the story, in fact the whole show.

To guard against such a mishap, I sprayed a thick gelatin-like liquid over the mask so the actor could then "fight" it. The liquid base prevented any smearing of the mask's features.

The ears were separate little foam latex appendages.

The hands were formed of some pieces I had left over (!) from another make-up job on a previous show.

The neck was effected by painting on spirit gum, laying absorbent cotton (with the fibers running horizontally) on it, and pressing it on till the whole gummed area was covered. Over the thin layer of cotton fiber a surgical adhesive was spread with a sponge. The neck was kept stretched till the whole thing dried, then the head lowered to normal position and, lo! the neck "aged" into a whole mass of realistic wrinkles.

The foregoing technique can also be used on the face to give it that "instant century" look in case you want to make yourself appear anywhere from 100 to 500 years older.

Last step: powder the area with a make-up which has a *castor* oil base. WARNING: the castor oil powder is not to be applied internally or you'll *really* have a sick green face!

MONSTERS
ARE
BADDER
THAN EVER

the beast is none too good for monsterama fans. the shape of things to come is reported in this exclusive story — just flown in by carrier-bat.

Alice just got back from Monsterland. She flew in on a beautiful, winged black nightmare. After taking a shower in lactic acid to clear away the cobwebs of her journey, she was ready to meet the ladies and gentlemen of the press.

She received the reporters in her swank apartment at Spectral Arms. Only ghost writers were allowed, of course, and had to present their cards at the door in order to be passed in by the in-spectre.

Once in, they almost passed out.

This singing man from THE MUMMY'S CURSE (with Lon Chaney Jr.) seems to be saying: "Ouch, you're squeezing my tonsils too hard. If you don't cut that out, I'll pour some water on that dusty old 3000-year-old body of yours and turn you into an Instant Mud Pie!"

91

We wonder who was the most scared, this beauty winner or the giant tarantula when they met up in TARANTULA?

brain in orbit

From the ceiling hung the first American *Spooknik*. Unlike the Soviet satellite, with its Lassie called Laika, no dog was in this sputnik but the world's most famous brain.

Donovan's brain!

Floating above the reporters, making mental notes on

The man with the hard-boiled egg eyes is out of KILLERS FROM SPACE. His eyes weren't always like that—it's just that on his planet they don't have any Marilyn Monroe, so can you blame his eyes for popping when he first saw an Earth calendar-girl?

everything that was said.

And so, by special arrangement with Alice von Wunderland and Don O-Van (the brain), FAMOUS MONSTERS OF FILMLAND takes great pride in bringing you, our readers, this glowing report on What's New in Monsterdom, hot off the wires. We know the wires were red-hot because we touched one of them. Can anybody use a toasted set of fingerprints?

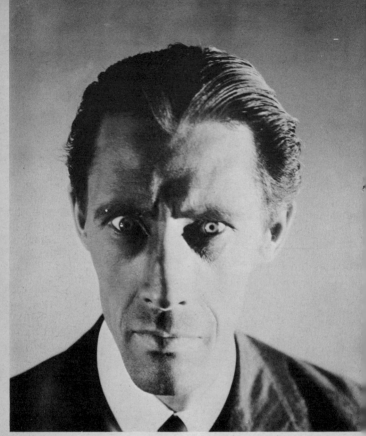

"Do you think you can outstare me? Even Fred couldn't, and he's as good Astaire'r as anybody!" (John Carradine)

the purple people-eater burps again

Have you noticed that Creatures are getting more colorful than ever? How about those starfish-shaped things from the stars with the big eye in their middle, THE MYSTERIANS?! And that man with the head of a thousand-eyed fly in THE FLY?! And—wowee!—that charm-boy in I MARRIED A MONSTER FROM OUTER SPACE, with the face that looks like he just washed it in spaghetti and can't do a thing with it?!

What next—*The Amazing Polka Dot Demon?* Well, there actually is a script being prepared called THE CRAZY

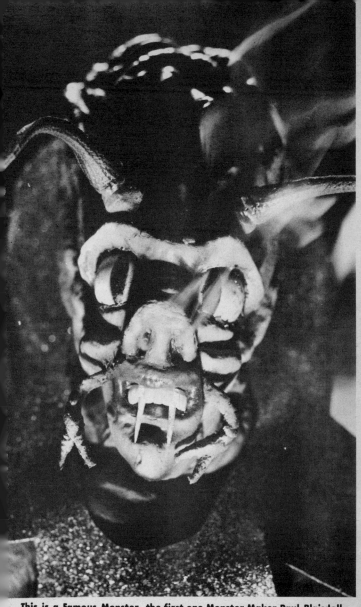

This is a Famous Monster—the first one Monster-Maker Paul Blaisdell ever built. "Herky," as he was called, is now spending his old age in the Museum of Retired Creatures.

95

Hello Hairy (Lon Chaney Jr.). Did you just wolf down another meal?

QUILT TERROR, and (believe it or not) they're going to make the first picture in 45rpm (roars per monster) called THE HIDEOUS ROCK 'N' ROLL CREATURE!!! But that's getting ahead of our story, into the Department of Predictions that comes at the end of this article.

(Now that you've been alerted, no fair peeking ahead a couple pages. Those pages have been coated with a special super-chemical that is ultra-sensitive

A friend like **TOBOR** the friendly robot is great for giving a guy a lift up, but he sure drinks a lot of oil to keep from getting rusty in his joints.

to peeking, and if you read the pages before you are supposed to, all the words will run together in a gooey mess.)

riding the horror cycle

Canny motion picture producers know a good thing when they see it, and they see it in the uncanny "bucks"-office returns of science-fiction and seance-fiction movies, so these studio bosses are riding horrocycles built not merely for two but designed to take a couple million thrill-seeking patrons for a ride thru Monsterland.

As Ray Parker recently put it in his syndicated column, "A whole new generation has discovered movie terror and fallen in love with monsters, things, creatures, super beasts, its, vampires, bats, saucermen, fiends, mutants, sea serpents, humanoids, bat men, cat women and teenage werewolves..

KING KONG has returned. DRACULA thirsts for blood. FRANKENSTEIN clanks again. Chances are that when Junior borrows the family car, he and his date will head for the drive-in theater that has the monster with three heads and a million eyes pursuing a teenage movie heroine through outer space."

Three heads—? Say, that Parker critter's got a real far out imagination. Nutty. Like they're just now making a movie about a man with *two* heads, and he comes up with *three!* How cool and cloudy can you get? Like, Ousterspaceville. I once met a cannibal whose Mother taught him that "too many cooks spoil the broth," so he never used cooks in his broth; and a Mutant with four eyes who agreed that two heads were better than *none*; but three—! Pass me the aspirin bottle like a good little monster, it gives me a headache just to think about it. When the heads on the

Peter Cushing and Robert Urquhart discuss a handy subject, such as making monsters in this scene from CURSE OF FRANKENSTEIN.

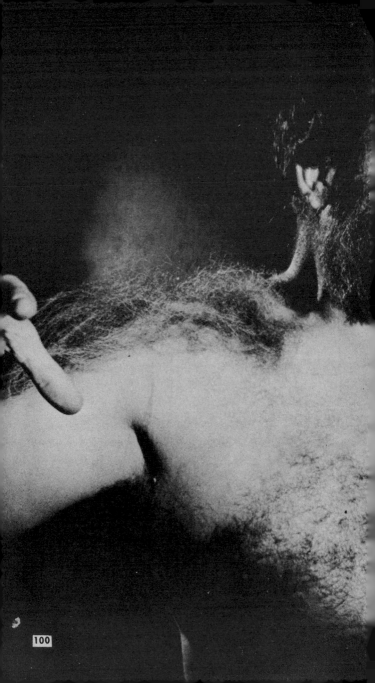

They call me one of THE UNEARTHLY. Against my parents' advice I started shaving when I was 12, and look what it did to my face.

outside get into an argument and make with the yakitty yak, do you suppose the one in the middle says, "Don't talk back!"?

run, do not creep

THE REVENGE OF FRANKENSTEIN, sequel to THE CURSE OF FRANKENSTEIN, was well worth seeing. The laboratory in particular was a real gasser; in fact, it was better than gas; it was electric. The whole theater was electrified when those floating eyes in the tank followed the light of the Bunsen burner like a moth attracted to a flame. If you missed this picture so far, don't wait for it to turn up on television, go out and track it down. Before it tracks *you* down. And if you can find it double-billed with the CURSE OF THE DEMON, so much the better, because CURSE OF THE DEMON is one of the really great supernatural pictures of all times, worthy to rate with the creepy CAT PEOPLE, the spooky DEAD OF NIGHT and the ghostly UNINVITED . . . not to overlook the macabre PICTURE OF DORIAN GRAY. That fire-breathing beast from the Devil's domain in CURSE OF THE DEMON is the hottest thing around lately. Dana Andrews' son Dave is a reader of this magazine and he told us that while his Dad was acting in that picture he didn't dare get too close to the monster's breath. We bit and asked him why, and he replied with a burst of maniacal laughter: "Because it's a *singe* he would have got toasted!" Gaargh, he got me! People who crack jokes like that should be invited over to a wienie roast, and they can be the wienie.

monsters growing by leaps and bounds

In 1956 there were 40 science-fiction and fantastic pix, many of them featuring monsters such as Blaisdell's BEAST WITH A MILLION EYES, Marla English as the seaweedy SHE-CREATURE, Bud Westmore's MOLE PEOPLE with their warty heads and knobby hands, the witch with the unbewitching face in the Spanish EL BRUJA, the goonish GAMMA PEOPLE, the monstrous GODZILLA from Japan, the Jekyll-Hydish HOMBRE Y LA BESTIA (MAN AND THE BEAST) from Mexico, the 3-eyed mutant in THE DAY THE WORLD ENDED, the throwbacks with the rundown faces in WORLD WITHOUT END and the oozing horror that was THE CREEPING UNKNOWN.

Last year the total was up a dozen titles. The huge mechanical monstrosity of KRONOS played hob on the

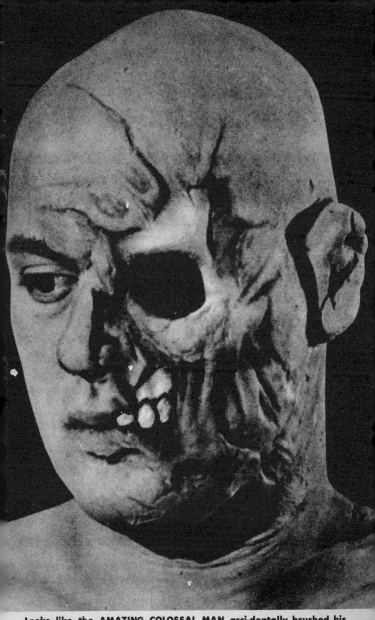

Looks like the AMAZING COLOSSAL MAN acci-dentally brushed his teeth too hard!

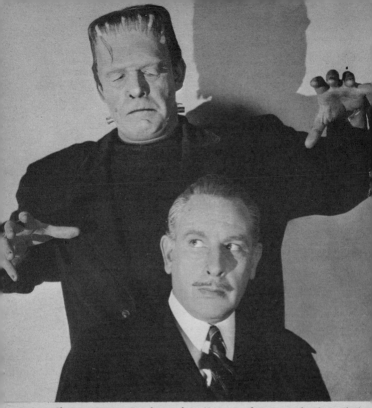

Lon Chaney Jr. as Frankenstein's Monster threatens the late Sir Cedric Hardwicke in this scene from Universal's GHOST OF FRANKENSTEIN.

screen ... the super sea-slug that was THE MONSTER THAT CHALLENGED THE WORLD wormed its way thru hackle-raising reels ... THE BLACK SCORPION gave its giant sting of death ... the pale creatures clomped in ZOMBIES OF MORA TAU, VOODOO ISLAND, THE MAN WHO TURNED TO STONE ... the mummies and werewolves and whatnots (beware the Whatnots!) were out in force in VOODOO WOMAN, THE UNDEAD, PHARAOH'S CURSE, THE VAMPIRE, TEENAGE MONSTER, I WAS A TEENAGE WEREWOLF, BACK FROM THE DEAD, etc. People generally put "etc." when they can't think of anything else to add. You think we ran out of titles? Ha! How about CAT GIRL, the supernatural thriller about the strange attachment between the heroine and a leopard? THE UNEARTHLY, which was *loaded* with

Exclusive! Scoop!! Confidential!!! FAMOUS MONSTERS OF FILMLAND brings you the first photograph of Inside Frankenstein! That's Basil Rathbone shining the x-ray machine on Boris Karloff's chest in SON OF FRANKENSTEIN, while broken-necked Ygor (Bela Lugosi) shows concern at the right.

monster-men and co-starred John Carradine and Tor Johnson? THE BODY IS A SHELL—the spiritualistic story of the survival of the soul after death? THE LIVING IDOL —Aztec reincarnation, with this time a girl concerned with a tiger rather than a leopard?

There was THE LAND UNKNOWN, loaded with flying pterodactyls with a wingspread as wide as an airplane, plus great prehistoric beasts of both land and lagoon.

There was MANBEAST, the shaggy menace of the Himalayas, the towering Abominable Snowman.

The crabby monsters (what else?) of ATTACK OF THE CRAB MONSTERS.

The city-wrecking DEADLY MANTIS.

The giant grasshoppers of THE BEGINNING OF THE END.

105

The one-eyed ogre called THE CYCLOPS.

The lava-like, radioactive mudpie-on-the-move that bubbled up from beneath the earth's crust and threatened to engulf the whole world in X, THE UNKNOWN.

THE NIGHT THE WORLD EXPLODED the only thing that kept its heroine, Kathy Grant, from going all to pieces was the thought that she would soon be Mrs. Bing Crosby!

monster great in '58

This was the Year of the Monsters. Monster lovers never had it so good. A magazine all your own, and a million movies (well, at least 75).

Leading all the rest, of course, is HOW TO MAKE A MONSTER, Herman Cohen's contribution to Monster Unlimited, with the She-Creature, the Cat Girl, the Voodoo Woman, the 3-eyed Mutant, the Teenage Frankenstein and a dozen other American-International horrors all rolled up into one tremonstrous package! No fewer than 17 frightening faces. The picture guaranteed to make you come out of the theater satisfied with your own ugly mug.

RETURN OF DRACULA and HORROR OF DRACULA shriek for themselves. By the way. Canadian readers: the picture known in your country as BLOOD OF THE DEMON was known here as BLOOD OF DRACULA; while you vampire fans over in England saw the same picture under the title of BLOOD IS MY HERITAGE! While we're on the subject of title changes, it might be interesting to note that in England THE INVASION OF THE SAUCER-MEN was titled INVASION OF THE HELL CREATURES, while ZOMBIES OF MORA TAU became THE DEAD THAT WALK! But let's not get too deep into that or we'll never get unmixed-up: in France the gi-ant picture THEM! was retitled THE MONSTERS ARE ATTACKING THE TOWN, and in Germany THIS ISLAND EARTH became METALUNA DOES NOT ANSWER.

How'd you like the "combination between a scorpion and a spider" as one reviewer described the FIEND WITHOUT A FACE? (And did they mix up the title in your local paper and call it *FRIEND* WITHOUT A FACE or FIEND *FROM OUTER SPACE?*) Another reviewer thought those flying brains resembled "winged hamburgers"; it must be admitted that when they were bashed by bullets, it looked like ketchup had been added. Deep-frozen spaghetti was more my idea of it.

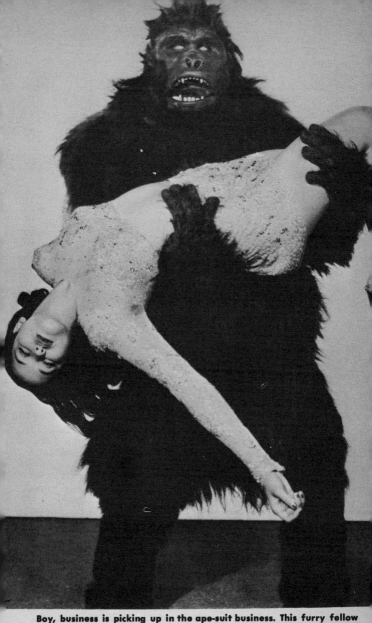

Boy, business is picking up in the ape-suit business. This furry fellow obviously has a job that suits him in CAPTIVE WILD WOMAN.

THE BEAST WITH A MILLION (count 'em) EYES—and all of them blood-shot. We wouldn't put it past him to attack that famous Tower in Paris—you know, the Eye-ful!

Bet you didn't know FIEND WITHOUT A FACE was written before any teenager in the audience was born—but a teenager wrote it! She was Amelia Reynolds Long, a woman still living, who had her story published in 1930 under the title "The Thought-Monster." The editor, now dead, described it as "a goose-flesh story of the sudden and frightful deaths caused by a strange creature in a panic-stricken village." In the original story the scientist recorded in his notes: "I shall create a mental being by the concentrated power of pure thought!" As you probably noticed, the story was brought up to date with an atomic background.

the man who lost his head

How about that crazy THING THAT COULD NOT DIE, huh? A head looking for a body for 400 years, the head of Gideon Drew, a 16th century delinquent who had too much to do with the Devil. Old Francis Drake himself (call him Sir!) took it upon himself to separate bad-boy

Drew from his body, and thereby hangs a—tale? Anyway, as tales go THE THING THAT COULD NOT DIE is a pretty tall one. All it needed was a revival of the old pop tune, "I Ain't Got No Body!"

Have you caught WAR OF THE COLOSSAL BEAST yet! THE AMAZING COLOSSAL MAN is in even worse shape in this follow-up film than he was in the first one.

Did MACABRE scare the daylights out of you? Did you burn the night lights for a week after seeing it? Did you meet up with anybody who collected the $10,000 Lloyds of London insurance policy by dying of fright during the picture?

I guess you noticed the big brother of Cecil the seasick sea serpent in THE SAGA OF THE VIKING WOMEN AND THEIR VOYAGE TO THE WATERS OF THE GREAT SEA SERPENT. And the mechanical brother of Frankenstein in THE COLOSSUS OF NEW YORK.

the shape of things to come!

A whole new crop of screamy pictures is due to scare you before year's end.

Personally, we're looking forward to THE CREATURE FROM GALAXY 27. This picture was written by Martin

Lon Chaney Jr. grabs Bela Lugosi by the collar, but Lugosi as Frankenstein's Monster doesn't seem too concerned with Chaney's threats.

Varno, a young Hollywood writer and actor himself just out of his teens so that he remembers very well what youthful monsterians go for, and you should go for this movie when it gets to your neighborhood. The monster itself is a kind of wingless bird-man with an enormous beak and ferocious claws. Marty wrote the screenplay in record time, and expects to do many more, eventually acting in, directing and producing his own motion pictures. So remember the name of an ex-teenager making good, and watch for further movies by Martin Varno.

Another hot one to watch for is TERROR FROM THE SUN, a new variation on the Jekyll-Hyde theme wherein Robert Clarke (producer, director and star) becomes a solar saurian, or sun-demon. The climax takes place atop one of Los Angeles' 300 foot high gas storage tanks. A new monster artist, Richard Cassarino, has created a reptile-man make-up to rival the Gill Man!

"Say buddy, I just ripped my new tweed overcoat. Can you recommend a good place for invisible mending?" "Try the Yellow Pages," replies John Carradine in THE INVISIBLE MAN'S REVENGE.

110

THE CREATURE FROM THE BLACK LAGOON seeks Revenge on the wise guy who put chlorine in his tank.

ATTACK OF THE BLOOD-LEECHES is calculated to make you feel anemic for days afterward. This is the one that Burt Shonberg designed. By the way, any of you FAMOUS MONSTER OF FILMLAND readers who ever find yourself in Laguna Beach, Calif., drop in and see Burt at his coffee-&-coke house called Café Frankenstein (This is for real.) Just mention that you read about his café with the monster murals and flying saucer paintings in this magazine and Burt will see to it that you get the king-size dish for your hot blood sundae. (Refills on iced blood are free—provided the blood comes from your own veins.)

DEBBIE AND THE DEMON has been tailored by the team of Larry Maddock & Corrie Howard, with Jack Seaman, to appeal to teeners. There's a real cute rock 'n' roll type junior demon who raises a lot of heck in the picture, plus a genuinely terrifying, old-as Methuselah demon.

If you watch closely in EARTH vs THE GIANT SPIDER,

111

in one scene you'll see one of the actors reading a copy of the Collector's Edition of the first issue of this magazine! Bert I. Gordon, producer of the picture (he also produced THE FANTASTIC PUPPET PEOPLE, THE CYCLOPS and the AMAZING COLOSSAL MAN duo) was so interested in FAMOUS MONSTERS OF FILMLAND MAGAZINE that he thought everyone who'll see his latest picture ought to know about it, so he put it in the film.

Only once in film history: two pictures playing at the same time that are such "naturals" to put together on the same double bill: THE SPIDER and THE FLY!

Kurt Neumann (who did ROCKETSHIP XM, SHE-DEVIL and KRONOS) has directed THE FLY, this shocker about the scientist who gets his own head replaced by that of a fly in human size, and it is not for the squeamish.

IT—THE VAMPIRE FROM OUTER SPACE and THE CURSE OF THE FACELESS MAN will be paired for the stronghearted. Jerome Bixby, veteran of 60 science-fiction stories, wrote the screenplays of these thrillers. VAMPIRE is about a blood-drinking monstrosity from another world loose on a spaceship far from earth; CURSE is about a man of Pompeii, buried alive during the eruption of Mt. Vesuvius, who returns to life after centuries in suspended animation.

mystavision

More creepy pictures are coming out soon than you could shake a broomstick at. This October you can really celebrate Horrorween in style by going to a new spook show. The Studios are working overtime so that by this Thanksgiving you'll really have something to be thankful for.

Run your thirsty eyeballs over this lovely list of tongue-talizing titles:

THE MONSTER.

MONSTER IN THE NIGHT.

THE TWO-HEADED MONSTER. (Suggested sequel: the first cowboy horror film, called THE TWO-HEADED MONSTER GOES WEST. Can't you just see him "headed" that-a-way ? ? ?)

THE PHANTOM PEOPLE.

THE SCREAMING SKULL (an American-International special).

THE BRAIN SNATCHERS.

See, *somebody*peekedwhentheyweren'tsupposedto — either-YOUorsomebodywhobrowsedthroughthismagazinebeforeyou— andtheamazingdetecto - chemicalformulaknownas*SuperSquish* instantlyreactedandallthewordsrantogetherjustlikeIwarnedy o u on page1O

Donald Wolfit examines a strange elixer in this scene from BLOOD OF THE VAMPIRE.

THE BEAST FROM WORLD'S END (introducing Budd Bankson's brain-children—and plenty chilly "children"—Chookne and Trog.

NIGHT OF THE BLOOD BEAST (another A-1 special).

HORRORS OF THE BLACK MUSEUM ... Cinema-Scope and color, story by Herman Cohen.

THE MAN WITHOUT A BODY (an English importation).

I BURY THE LIVING (man driven to the verge of madness by the suspicion that he has the power to send people to an untimely death).

BLACK PANIC.

THE HOUSE ON HAUNTED HILL.

THE CREEPING HORROR.

The first Italian-made sci-fi horror film, DEATH COMES FROM SPACE.

A one-man horror show, Alex Gordon, tells me that he almost single-handedly will fill up the screen with a full slate of horror, sci-fi and monster movies. For FAMOUS MONSTERS OF FILMLAND readers Mr. Gordon confided to your editor that he plans to produce:

1. THE PROJECTED MAN, an original screenplay about a lethally electric human menace.

2. THE HOUND OF HELL, a horror yarn by Gordon's beautiful and talented wife, known professionally as Ruth Alexander.

3. THE INVISIBLE MONSTER.

4. THE WHISPERING GHOUL.

5. A new version of Robert Louis Stevenson's classic of terror, THE SUICIDE CLUB.

6. THE MASK OF THE RED DEATH, adapted by Ruth Alexander from Edgar Allan Poe's shuddersome short story.

7. THE TERROR THAT STALKED AT NIGHT.

Quite a schedule, and a real treat for the quiver-&-quake crowd!

karloff and frankenstein

And, of course, the greatest monster thrills imaginable are in store with Boris Karloff himself in:

CORRIDORS OF BLOOD!

THE DOCTOR OF 7 DIALS!

And—KING OF THE MONSTERS!

While the latest Frankenstein film, FRANKENTEIN'S DAUGHTER and FRANKENSTEIN—1970, are to be followed by another Technicolor spectacle from the producers of THE CURSE OF FRANKENSTEIN and THE REVENGE OF FRANKENSTEIN: FRANKENSTEIN CREATED WOMAN!

The Face in the Tombstone Mirror will be the first in the new teleseries of Tales of Frankenstein, authored shortly before his tragic death by the late Henry Kuttner. Second in the series, *Frankenstein Meets Dr. Varno,* has been prepared by Jerome Bixby, co-author of THE HURRICANE MAN.

House of Wax is serving as the basis of a terrorvision series for the video channels. Horror master Curt Siodmak is working out a package of terrifying tales for TV called *Black Orchid Garden.*

So, as the Latins said, it's plainly a case of "Monsters for All."

The *shape* of Things to Come is mysterious, mutant, macabre and monsterful.

Your editor ought to know. How?

My Monster Done Tol' Me!   END

"Hello, my name's Shock Hudson. I'm THE MONSTER FROM OUTER SPACE that my wife married. Where I come from I'm considered terribly handsome. Would you believe I have more fans than Clark Ghoulble?"

Robots of the World, Arise! You're as good
as other guys! You can outdo all Man's
plans, tho your parents were tin cans.

21st Century Poem attributed to
Koyle Chapeque, Poet Laureate of Toboria

METAL MONSTERS

It was 40 years ago that the world first heard of robots. They began in Czechoslovakia, in the mind of sci-fi author and playwright, Karel Capek. He created them for his play *R.U.R—Rossum's Universal Robots.* Any dictionary worth its name will tell you where "robot" came from, but how many well-educated individuals realize that, by definition, Capek didn't create robots after all—his brain gave birth *to androids!*

117

Modern Golems!

Humanoids!

For the popular concept of a Robot has come to be a man of metal, a creation of cooper and steel and wires and light bulbs.

An automaton.

A Tobor.

A Robby.

METROPOLIS, the wonder film of the century, the

Syko, the Mad Mechanical Man. Played by Robot Bloch. (From Universal Serial THE VANISHING SHADOW, 1934.)

movie of a million marvels, 35 years ago brought to the screen the most compelling robot the world has ever seen. It was, to fall back on a cliche, "a thing of beauty and a joy forever." True, Rotwang the mad inventor, put this marvelous mechanism to evil use, but that does not alter the basic fact of its esthetic fascination.

The Metropolis Robot (or *robotrix*, for it was fashioned in feminine form) stood human high and was a stream-lined symphony of shining steel. Only its pinpoint eyes betrayed the slightest hint that there might be something

Bang! And another robot bit the dust. Now pour water on him and he'll bite the rust! (EARTH vs. THE FLYING SAUCERS, 1956.)

Hm, a very human robot, chasing the pretty girl as usual. All he really wants is a cup of oil. (From Mexican movie PLATILLOS VOLA-DORES: FLYING SAUCERS.)

sinister connected with it; otherwise, audiences thrilled to its contours like the shapes of things to come: the fins and fishtails of fashionable cars, the serpentine elegance of modern lamps, the sleek lines of lunarbound rockets.

The Metrobot remains unequalled, unsurpassed.

the metro-goldwyn robot

But—temporalily skipping all robots in between—30 years later MGM perfected a robot so pleasing to the public that "he" not only stole the show in FORBIDDEN PLANET but threatened to become as durable a character as The Creature from the Black Lagoon, the Mummy or the In-visable Man. He was, as anyone over the age of 8 well knows, Robby the Robot, who after his debut in the interstellar thriller about Altair IV was called back for

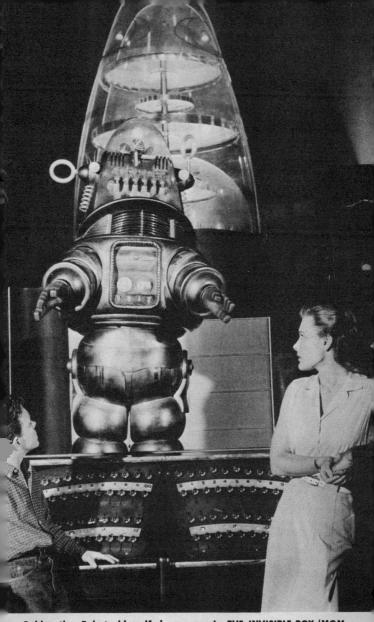

Robby the Robot, himself, in person. In THE INVISIBLE BOY (MGM 1957).

CAPTAIN VIDEO meets mechanical servant of the baddies from planet Atoma. We doubt this particular robot would frighten a 2-year-old. No doubt one of our 2-year-old readers will write us on this score; FM has very smart readers.

further service in THE INVISIBLE BOY and even involved in a play in a telepisode of *The Thin Man!*

Robby became not only a household word, he became a household *pet* in many homes where the toymakers of America found ready acceptance for miniature models of this most famous of all modern mechanical men.

But if Robby and the Metrobot had their endearing qualities, it must be admitted, quantitywise, that most movie robots have been revolting.

Take the Tin Can Man of TARGET-EARTH!: a real troublemaker. A soldier of steel sent from Venus, complete with death-ray. Unfortunately, however, this robot was so unconvincingly constructed that it generated fear in no one, unless it was the backers of the picture that they wouldn't get their money back. This "warrior" robot looked like little other than a discarded collection of cans built around a big barrel, with a man inside. As the robot's ray operated on hi-fry (high-frequency) kill-o-psycho's, legend has it that the man inside the robot was Robert Bloch, a speculation he has never bothered to deny and which, as it corresponded with the shooting time of the picture, *would* explain that mysterious 2-weeks absence of his from Rossum Jr. High.

TOBOR THE GREAT was an anthropomorphical servo-mechanism. You know it's true or we wouldn't publish it in FM. But since only King Kong has a mouth big enough for a mouthful like that, we'll run it thru our special Translation Machine to find out what it means. The Robotranslator says: *Tobor is Robot spelled backwards; "he" was made in human form to serve man.* Ah, now we have it. In the picture, Tobor was designed to replace a human pilot on the pioneer trip to the Moon. But enemy agents sabotaged the moonflight by can-napping Tobor (that's the way you kidnap a metal man; no kidding) and turning him against his inventor, a la Frankenstein. Would you call a metal Frankestein a Crankenstein? No, we didn't think you would; only the twisted *niarb* (that's a backward brain) of an Ackermanoid robot would pull such a horrible *nup* as that!

By popular demand of Rossum's Universal Rabbits (they're hare-brained robots) we will bring you Part 2 in *The Robot Story* in a near future issue, "The Return of Android Hardy," wherein you will find fotos and discussions of the metal monsters of GOG, DEVIL GIRL FROM MARS, THE PHANTOM EMPIRE, THE BIG COMET, THE DAY THE EARTH STOOD STILL and others.

Tell your friends!

Tell your enemies!

Tell your favorite robot!

Careful, Tobor, there's a $25 fine for hitting a man with glasses.
From TOBOR THE GREAT, 1954.

END

125

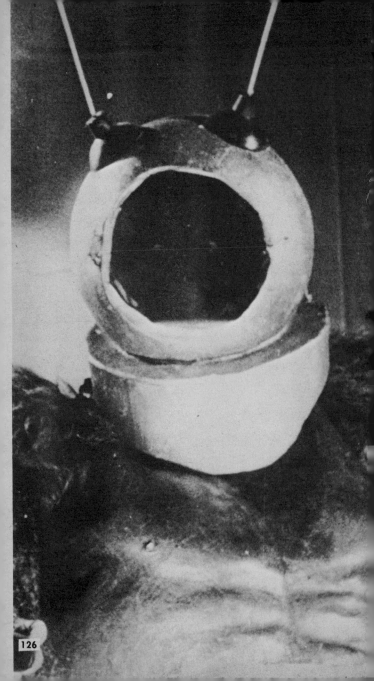

I WAS A TIN AGE ROBOT

The Conclusion of The Robot Story

A True Confession
by McKanical Mann

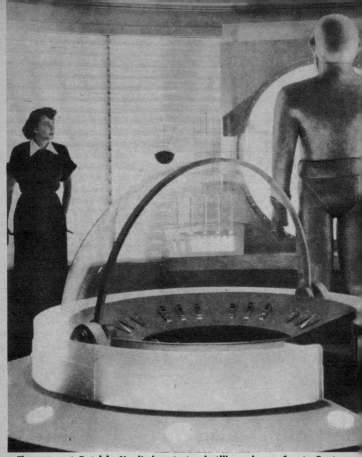

The moment Patricia Neal's heart stood still, as she confronts Gort, the metallic creation from another world, invincible servant and bodyguard of Michael Rennie in THE DAY THE EARTH STOOD STILL (20th-Fox, 1951).

Robot Mitchum was my Father. Gear Garson was my Mother. McConnie-gal Francis was my first girlfriend.

My great grandmother was the original can-can girl and my grandfather was the first metal man employed in an automobile repair shop.

My uncle Hum-Bolt constructed the first Iron Curtain. We used it in our home to keep the bathroom dry when we took a shower. Of course, we always showered in oil, as all robots hate water like vampires loathe wolfbane. Rust, you know. We went oily to bed and oily to rise.

Two strange visitors from Outer Space. On the left is Klaatu (Michael Rennie) and with him is Gort. Both of these individuals seem intent on one purpose—making the Earth stand still.

129

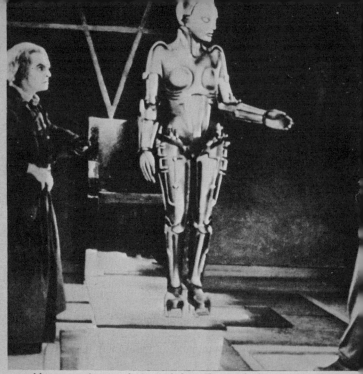

In this extremely rare photograph from the classic silent masterpiece **METROPOLIS**, Rotwang the scientist demonstrates his greatest invention, the Robotrix, for the benefit of a friend.

gort the great

One of my happiest childhood experiences, as a young boybot, was being taken by my aunt, Elizabeth Toiler, together with my cousin, Tuesday Welder, to see THE DAY THE EARTH STOOD STILL. That was back in 1951, when 20th-Fox did this great job on Gort, the splendid steelman from another world who arrived via saucership as a companion to Michael Rennie. Tuesday said she could have gotten a crush on Michael if he'd only been a robot; "why couldn't he have been McOil Rennie?" she sighed. Be that as it may, it was a great day for robotdom when the earth stood still.

GOG wasn't bad either, altho quite different in construction from Gort. Whereas Gort resembled human beings, Gog had half a dozen arms—2 in front, 2 in back and 2

Time for a coffee break on Altair Four, as Robby the Robot plays host in this scene from FORBIDDEN PLANET.

on both sides (a much more convenient arrangement than human beings) — and moved about on a tractor principle rather than clumsy legs. Altogether an improvement over people, I'd say. Too bad the badski's got control of him and made him do mean things so that the scientists weren't his friends any more and destroyed him.

kronos, colossus, diabolicus!

The giant robot in COLOSSUS OF NEW YORK was quite a guy with his weird voice-box and eyes that flashed on and off when he talked. Of course, he had a human brain in him, and that's kind of no fair; I mean, like how would a human being like a monkey's brain in *his* head?

"Diabolicus" (that's just a name I made up) was the metal servant of the DEVIL GIRL FROM MARS, and he was pretty diabolical, alright, as you can see from his picture. KRONOS, of course, was the King Kong of mechanical

131

menaces. Robot, was he big! Some critics had the audacity to call him a super Tinkertoy but as a teenbot of about 16 he sure brought joy to the heart—I mean my plastic ticker. It really made my electric circuits flash when Kronos went thumping up and down the countryside, leveling towns, smashing automobiles and turning people into instant jello!

from murania to uraania

Dad never tires of telling me how, when he was a kidbot, he went to the theater every Saturday afternoon (disguised as a prize in a crackerjack box) to see installments of a serial called THE PHANTOM EMPIRE, all about a super-scientific civilization in an underground world called Mu-

TOBOR THE GREAT rides again. This time with the assistance of a Jeep in this scene from the Republic film of 1954.

Ralph Morgan is caught in the clutches of a Robot monster in this scene from the Columbia serial THE MONSTER AND THE APE.

rania. Dad says that some of our relatives got work in the picture, playing Tin Woodsman type robots.

And tho I didn't see the picture, a correspondent of mine in Sweden (Swedish steel is the best, you know) tells me his countrymen made a sci-fi comedy a couple years ago called JOHNNY VENGMAN AND THE BIG COMET. "And what do you think was in it?" ask my friend Hans Siden. (He's a good boy, for a human.) "A robot!" He even sent a picture to prove it.

Lastly but not leastly I suppose I should mention that beastly TWONKY, that kookie Kuttnerian model of a television set that cut up such capers on celluloid that for awhile we were afraid people were almost going to shoot every TV on sight, and some of our best pets are videos.

recapitulation

So, to sum up, here's a record of every movie we can ever remember seeing or hearing of that in some way, *shape or form* had something to do with robots, androids, humanoids or adenoids. (Now, let's get nosey!)

THE ROBOT STORY

AELITA

CAPTAIN VIDEO

THE COLOSSUS OF NEW YORK

THE DAY THE EARTH STOOD STILL

DEVIL GIRL FROM MARS

EARTH vs. THE FLYING SAUCERS

FORBIDDEN PLANET

GOG

THE GOLEM(S)

THE INVISIBLE BOY

JOHNNY VENGMAN AND THE BIG COMET

KRONOS

METROPOLIS

LA MOMIA CONTRA EL ROBOT HUMANO

THE MYSTERIANS

THE PHANTOM EMPIRE

ROBOT MONSTER

TARGET—EARTH!

TOBOR THE GREAT

THE TWONKY

THE UNDERSEA KINGDOM

VAMPIRES OVER LONDON

THE VANISHING SHADOW

Perhaps YOU can add to the list?   END

This robot, THE COLOSSUS OF NEW YORK, had a human brain. (From Wm. Alland's production for Paramount, 1958).

BOYS WILL BE

Boys Will Be Beasts! That's the motto of the Mad Make-up Man of Scramerican-Uttergnahnal Studios, which is a good place to stay

BEASTS

away from unless you want to become a Teenage Werewolf and a Teenage Frankenstein!

END 137

KING OF ALL THE

MONSTERS

by Forrest J Ackerman

BORIS KARLOFF granted me an interview & it is my pleasure to share it with you.

Karloff as Dr. Frankenstein examines a pair of new eyes for his new monster. (FRANKENSTEIN 1970.)

Next to Lon Chaney Sr., whom I never met, for years the man in monsterdom that I most wanted to meet was Boris Karloff. It was not enough that I had once seen him briefly backstage after a performance in ON BORROWED TIME and acquired his autograph on a copy of the anthology he engineered, "And the Darkness Falls". It was not enough that once in my life I saw Peter Lorre, stood next to Charles Laughton, watched Lon Chaney Jr. act, observed Basil Rathbone on a set, regarded a funeral bed on which Colin

Karloff and Lugosi as they appeared in the Universal classic SON OF FRANKENSTEIN (1939).

Clive lay dead, called Tor Johnson "friend", have seen Elsa Lanchester & Rod Serling & Fritz Lang & Brigitte Helm & John Carradine & Fredric March (Dr. Jekyll) & Spencer Tracy (Mr. Hyde) in person, been in Vincent Price's home, saw Dwight Frye on the stage in DRACULA, and that Bela Lugosi & I were friends while the final curtain was slowly

Karloff starred with Charles Laughton, Raymond Massey and Ernest Thesiger in THE OLD DARK HORSE.

descending on his life.

No, above all else I always wanted to really *meet* Boris Karloff, to converse with him a short time, to express my appreciation to him for the pleasure he has given me in the past 30 years.

Jim Nicholson of American-International was thoughtful

Boris reads the Sacred Scroll of Toth in the role of 3700 year old Im-Ho-Tep in Universal's classic, THE MUMMY.

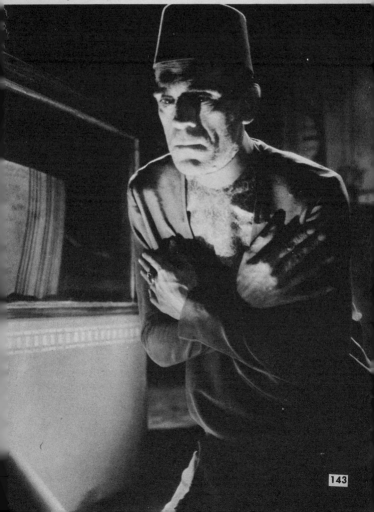

143

As the Monster, in SON OF FRANKENSTEIN.

enough to arrange it for me late last year. It was during the filming of THE RAVEN. Sam Sherman, our editorial director of *SCREEN THRILLS ILLUSTRATED*, was visiting Hollywood from New York, and I took him along to the studio with me. It was Sam who first spotted Karloff. He suddenly nudged me & said, "There he goes now. Now's your opportunity. You can catch him in his dressingroom."

I met my favorite

I high-tailed it to the cubicle into which Mr. Karloff had just vanished. He had just eased himself into a chair when I approached the open door of the little room and, placing one foot on the first stair & inserting my head part way into the room, I asked, "Would it be all right to come in a moment?"

He was very gracious. "Why, yes, of course," he said,

B.K.—Today. Long live the King!

As THE GHOUL (1934)

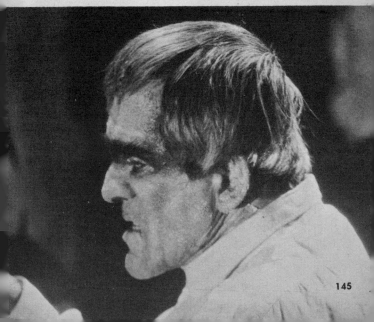

145

In the 1934 classic, THE BLACK CAT.

As a master of magic and sorcery in AIP's THE RAVEN.

his world-famous voice sounding just as it had in THE BLACK CAT, THE INVISIBLE RAY, THE MUMMY and so many others.

I introduced myself as the editor of FAMOUS MONSTERS. "I have a set of your magazines," he replied. This neither flattered nor surprised me as I had visited the set a few days earlier, missed him, and left the magazines in a package on a table for him.

"I have enjoyed your pictures for over 30 years," I said. "Since FRANKENSTEIN—that was about 1931, wasn't it?"

"Yes," he said, "that was about the beginning of it." I knew that, historically speaking, his statement was far from accurate, for it is recorded that as early as 1916 (in fact the year I was born) he appeared in a picture, THE DUMB GIRL OF PORTICI ... in 1919 was in the Doug Fairbanks film HIS MAJESTY, THE AMERICAN ... acted in Kosmik Films' 15-part serial THE HOPE DIAMOND MYSTERY in 1921 and, the same year, appeared in THE CAVE GIRL ... etc. However, I knew what he meant, that figuratively speaking his career began with his immortal portrayal of the Frankenstein monster, and I did not make a point of questioning his statement.

Just then someone opened the door & called him away momentarily to answer the phone. I took advantage of his temporary absence to soak in the atmosphere, to realize that I was sitting in *the dressingroom of Boris Karloff* and that in a few minutes he, like his indestructible monster, would return!

the return of karloff

When Mr. Karloff did indeed return, I asked him about THE BELLS. "Ah, yes," he replied, "the silent film with Lionel Barrymore. I played a strange physician in it, a practitioner of mesmerism." We might have discussed the picture & other of his early performances but at that moment another individual appeared at his door, a man who turned out to be a mutual friend, producer Alex Gordon. As I recall (and it is too late at 2 o'clock in the·morning as I type these words to call & double check it) Alex' brother produced the British Karloffilm CORRIDORS OF BLOOD that is about to be released in this country. Alex & Boris chatted briefly & then it was time for Mr. Karloff to enact a scene—Roger Corman was calling for him on the set.

the shock of my life

I have seen Karloff in roles like the original RAVEN where he was quite twisted and THE TOWER OF LONDON where he had the bandy legs & club foot and in THE BLACK ROOM but from his TV appearances as host of *Thriller* I

As Dr. Niemann in the HOUSE OF FRANKENSTEIN.

thought of him as standing quite erect, very tall & straight. It was, therefore, a terrific shock to me to observe how truly bent he is in real life. It seemed to me that, walking naturally, he was almost more doubled over, more crablike in his appearance, than I had ever seen him when putting on an act on the screen. At that moment I felt a great compassion for him; in a telepathic world he would have heard in his head a sincerely meant message from me that would have said, *"Dear* Mr. Karloff, much as I personally love you & want you to live forever & go on acting forever, *I* wouldn't ask you to go on acting at the age of 75." I wondered why he wasn't 6000 miles away with his wife, sitting comfortably in front of his hearth in his home in England, instead of here on this sound stage, about to climb, unaided, a steep flight of stairs, then have to clamber up some rubble.

The scene he was about to shoot was practically the end of the picture. It was just after the grand explosion following the duel of wizards. Dust & debris were still falling out of the air (studio workers studiously pumping vile vapors in his direction). He did the scene where he tried to repair or change a dress for his wife by a wave of his hand; unsuccessful, he bowed his head & said, "I guess I just don't have it any more."

A voice at my side spoke. I had been so engrossed in watching Boris Karloff act that for the moment I had half-forgotten the presence of my friend & fellow editor by my side. " . . . just don't have it any more" was echoing in my ears when Sam Sherman commented to me under his voice, "Oh *yes* he does!" And it is indeed true. At 75, Boris Karloff has lost none of his touch, his magic, his mesmeric attraction —if anything, I would say after witnessing his performance in THE RAVEN that he is more powerful than ever.

last minutes with my master

He autographed my photoplay edition of FRANKENSTEIN and let Sam & me pose for pictures with him, then he sat on a stool, reading some "wild lines," hamming it up, enjoying himself hugely & making me feel that apparently I was wrong in feeling concern about him. Despite his shortness of breath, the arthritis or whatever it is that curves him so cruelly, he obviously was having fun. Unlike Lugosi, that poor old narcotic-ruined shell of a man in the last years of his life, it is evident that Mr. Karloff does not have to keep going for financial reasons. Like today's elder statesman of singers, Maurice Chevalier, Boris Karloff evidently continues his motion picture & TV career primarily because he loves his work, his fans.

As the cruel master of BEDLAM.

Before flying back over the North Pole to home, he made one more picture now awaiting release: THE TERROR, in color.

If & when you read the lines of this interview, Mr. William Henry Pratt, I want again to say "thank you". My hat's off to you, my head's in the clouds & my heart's wishing you all the warmest. In these sentiments I'm sure well over a hundred thousand readers of this magazine simultaneously join me.

In chorus we say: *"O King, live forever!"* **END**

MAD
LABS
the labratory story!

Eric Von Stroheim performs an evil experiment in this scene from
THE CRIME OF DR. CRESPI.

lab at first sight

Consider: how could Franken ever have made a stein
without a laboratory?

Where would Donovan have parked his brain without a
laboratory?

Where would Dr. X have got all his fresh aches without
a lab? On his poultry earnings you have to hen it to him that
he made a down payment on his first test tube when he
was only 10. His first experiment: to go Nature one better

Peter Cushing carefully observes his scientific machinery in EVIL OF FRANKENSTEIN.

and, instead of getting down off a duck, get down off a hippopotamus. And trying to accomplish this was complicated by the fact that at the time he couldn't even spell hippopotamus, let alone climb up on one.

don't blab about the lab!

The first rule of the lab (it has been referred to as the Ghoulden Rule) is: *don't blab!*

That guy in THE FLY did, and lost his head.

Blabbermouths in Lugosian labs invariably lost their wives.

Spencer Tracy as Dr. Jekyll patiently waits for the serum which will transform him into the loathsome Mr. Hyde.

Talk-too-muchniks in Karloffian labs frequently lost their lives.

Of course every young assistant *must* work in a lab, else where would he meet the Scientist's Beautiful Daughter to whom he must inevitably lose his heart? The obvious advantage to losing your heart in a mad scientist's laboratory is that is never very difficult to get a fresh one.

the lab of the gods

In all seriousness, laboratories have been the hi-lite of many a memorable motion picture. The LaboraForry of

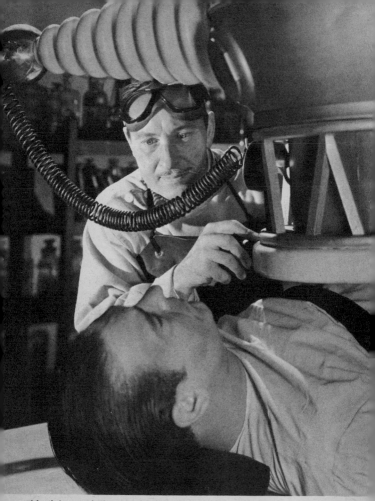

This lab specializes in Atomics, and Lionel Atwill is about to give atomic ache to THE ATOMIC MONSTER (Lon Chaney, Jr).

Dr. Ack's that lives on ever green in my mind after 30 years is the glorious Robot Room in METROPOLIS. There Rotwang, the mad one-handed inventor, very literally *single-handedly* created the unforgetable metal marvel, Maria the Automaton. Rotwang's magical laboratory was constructed with typical German thoroughness and titanic Teutonic imagination, and for my money (I'd give a lot of Deutsch Marks to have a duplicate of it) it's never been topped.

Anton Diffring tests a hypodermic needle before injecting his next victim. A scene from the teleseries TALES OF FRANKENSTEIN.

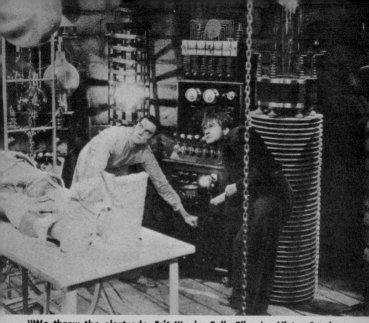

"We throw the electrode, Fritz!" cries Colin Clive (as Victor Frankenstein) to his assistant, Dwight Frye, as they make their successful try at bringing the FRANKENSTEIN monster to life in the first of the entire series.

plasant and accounted for

Also present and accounted for are such goodies in the way of labbies as:

James Whale's thrilling concept of the Frankenstein assembly-shop in the original film and its sequel, THE BRIDE...

The Jacob's-ladderatories of such derringdo serials as FLASH GORDON, BUCK ROGERS, THE LOST CITY and THE PHANTOM EMPIRE, where things really sparkled and hummed so electrifyingly that you imagined you could smell the ozone in the audience — years before the advent of Odorama or Schozzoscope....

Karloff's curious seance-fiction lab in the ectoplasmic DEVIL COMMANDS...

The multicolored labs of Dr. X and Lionel Atwill in THE MYSTERY OF THE WAX MUSEUM and the guy in THE FLY.

Just thinking about those labs makes my mouth water, how about you? Hungry for some popcorn? Meet you in the labby..!   **END**

MONSTERAMA

QUIZ

If your orbs have been in orbit while you have been getting an eyeful of the gleeful ghouls and mickey monsters in this issue of Have Monster, Will Grovel (alias FAMOUS MONSTERS), you should be able to answer all the questions right. If you make a single mistake, it must be because you bought a copy of the wrong monster magazine, and that was a grave mistake indeed.

Consider all questions carefully, and think twice before answering, especially if it is the doorbell ringing and it is a dark night: It might be Count Dracula, and then your life as well as his would be like a wooden stick thru the heart—at stake!

If you don't know the answers offhand, try off-claw.

It is perfectly permissable to purchase issues of FAMOUS MONSTER magazine in order to cram for the Quiz.

If you get all the questions correct, you may become Editor of FAMOUS MONSTERS. Then, again, you may not, as the editor needs to be fed to remain undead, and as Vampira once said, "It's a dying."

If you miss a question, don't confess your shame to your best friend at school the next day or he may not share his shocklate cake with you from his lunch pale.

If you miss ALL the questions, you are a GENIUS! Go down to the Memory Bank and make an immediate withdrawal. And if you lose your mind on the way, apply to the Lost & Fiend Dept.

NOW, TURN THE PAGE... 159

QUESTIONS

1. The star of HORROR OF DRACULA was: Christopher Lee, Christopher Columbus, Chris Kringle. Pick two (and throw away—only one is right).
2. MIGHTY JOE YOUNG was the son of: Robert Young? Loretta Young? Egg Foo Young?
3. True or false: I WAS A TIN AGE ROBOT was the sequel to CAN-CAN.
4. I WAS A HOT TAMALE was the sequel to THE SUN DEMON (true or false?)
5. TWENTY MILLION LEAGUES UNDER THE SEA was about a mermen's baseball team—true or false?
6. I BURY THE LIVING starred: Wallace Bury, Bury Ford, Razz Bury. (Tip: pick none!)
7. When THE INCREDIBLE SHRINKING MAN married THE DEVIL DOLL, the result was THE FANTASTIC PUPPET PEOPLE. Likely?
8. ABBOTT & COSTELLO MEET FRANKENSTEIN starred Martin & Lewis, Steve Allen & Ed Sullivan, Costello & Abbott. (What a cast!)
9. The theme song of THE BODY SNATCHERS was "You Gotta Have Heart!" (Yes or no?)
10. The theme song of SON OF KONG was "It Takes Two to Kong-a!" (Believe it or nut.)
11. THE INVISIBLE RAY was Ray Bradbury, Ray Lugosi, Ray Beam. (Who Ray?)
12. I WAS A STEIN AGE FRANK starred Frank Sinatra, Frank Lovejoy, Frank Furter. (Guess again.)
13. CRY OF THE FOOT BAWL was the changed title of THE PIGSKIN GHOUL. (Touchdown or fumble?)
14. THE RETURN OF THE SWAT was the sequel to what picture?
15. SEVEN BRIDES FOR SEVEN MUMMIES was based on a Broadway musi-ghoul show. (False note or true?)
16. THE INVISIBLE WOMAN was detected and captured because she talked a blue streak (true or false).
17. Gaga Gabor is the star of QUEEN OF OATER SPACE (true or false).
18. STINGS TO COME was the British title of THE BLACK SCORPION (true or false).
19. Tim Hovey starred in TOM SWIFT AND HIS ELECTRIC CHAIR (true or false).
20. This is the best issue yet of FAMOUS MONSTERS (no doubt!)

ANSWERS

1. Your choice of the three should be Mr. Lee.
2. Whoever his parents were, they sure made a monkey out of Joe.
3. Ask Rin-Tin-Tin.
4. There never was a picture called I WAS A HOT TAMALE. Did you bite on this one?
5. Don't look now, but you've just had your league pulled.
6. That's the last straw, Bury!
7. Well, don't you shrink so?
8. Who's on third?
9. Either that or "I Ain't Got No Body."
10. "Song of Kong" was based on the book, "Kong with the Wind."
11. Well, it wasn't Fay Wray.
12. It was Frank Lee O'Weiner.
13. This question was put in just for kicks. (And I bet I'll get 'em!)
14. THE FLY!
15. Mum's the word.
16. She was an acrobat's daughter, and when she opened her mouth she put her foot in it.
17. Yep, and it's the first picture about the wild oh-pun spaces.
18. Stung again!
19. False, it was ATOM SWIFT And His Electric HIGH CHAIR with Tom Hoovey.
20. Well, don't just stare there, prove it by buying a second issue for a friend. And if you don't have a friend, you'll make one by making him a present of FAMOUS MONSTERS!

Third Big Printing!

FOR THE FIRST TIME IN PAPERBACK!

THE BEST FROM

FAMOUS

MONSTERS

OF FILMLAND

Including over 150 spine-tingling photos

52-290, 50¢

AND

SON OF

FAMOUS

MONSTERS

OF FILMLAND

WITH OVER 150 RARE PHOTOS

52-504, 50¢

If you are unable to obtain these books from your local dealer, they may be ordered directly from the publisher.

PAPERBACK LIBRARY, INC.
Department B
260 Park Avenue South
New York, N.Y. 10010

Please send me the following books:
I am enclosing payment plus 10¢ per copy to cover postage and handling

Book # .... Title .... No. of copies ....
     # .... Title .... No. of copies ....
Name ....
Address ....
City ....
State ....